Cl
V

Volkswagen
Motors
1948-1968

Richard Copping

Nostalgia Road Publications

CONTENTS

The Nostalgia Road Series™

is produced under licence by

Nostalgia Road Publications Ltd.
Units 5-8, Chancel Place, Shap Road Industrial Estate,
Kendal, Cumbria, LA9 6NZ
Tel.+44(0)1539 738832 - Fax: +44(0)1539 730075

designed and published by

Trans-Pennine Publishing Ltd.
PO Box 10, Appleby-in-Westmorland, Cumbria, CA16 6FA
Tel.+44(0)17683 51053 Fax.+44(0)017683 53558
e-mail:admin@transpenninepublishing.co.uk

and printed by
Kent Valley Colour Printers Ltd.
Kendal, Cumbria +44(0)1539 741344

Front Cover: *What car could be featured on the front cover of a book about Volkswagen other than the Beetle? Love it or loath it, from a dark past the post-war Beetle became the best-known car in the world. Export was the key to its success and here in Britain VW first invaded officially in 1953, when just 945 cars were sold.*

Rear Cover Top: *The Karmann Ghia introduced in 1955 as a coupe and two years later as a convertible, caught the public's imagination thanks to the elegant Carrozzeria Ghia design, and despite its somewhat pedestrian and pure Beetle performance.*

Rear Cover Bottom: *The Transporter, Volkswagen's second model, made its debut in 1950 and in a short space of time a variety of guises became available, including the top of the range Microbus Deluxe with sunroof pictured. The Transporter revolutionised the world of the light commercial vehicle, inspired countless camper conversions and was a forerunner in the business of people carrying.*

Title Page: *'Volkswagenwerk AG Wolfsburg' as it looked at the end of the period covered by this book. Although the factory was no longer responsible for every VW built, and hadn't been since the emergence of first Hanover (Transporters) and later Emden (Beetles for the US market), it was the major contributor to a daily production level of 7,500 vehicles.*

This Page: *Although VWs brochures of the 1960s lacked the individuality of the previous decade, the photographers still produced shots worthy of attention.*

INTRODUCTION

Welcome to the world of the Volkswagen enthusiast – not just any old world, but rather specifically the years of air-cooled ascendancy; two golden decades with one man at the helm of what was initially a decidedly tin-pot empire, but which was rapidly to become one of Europe's premier money-earners; a company sporting a brand name instantly recognisable across the world.

Subsequent books will delve into the world of 'splits', 'ovals' and 'slopers' (to the uninitiated those are all 'types' of Beetle) or 'splitties', 'bays' and 'wedges' (VW's commercial vehicle) and even 'low light Ghias' and 'razor edges'. However, the purpose here is distinctly to 'overview this 20-year period,' while producing a light-hearted analysis of the firm's incredible success story.

For a self-confessed air-cooled addict to cover what happened after the death of Volkswagen's first post-war German Director General, Heinz Nordhoff, when the slow drip of water eventually became a torrent of Golfs, Polos and Passats could be an excruciating experience. Yet, as we will see in a later book some of these cars have become classics in their own right and were eventually to save VW from a near terminal canker, injected into the company's life-blood in 1968!

The scenario for this volume comes in several easy stages. The prelude centres on a crazy dictator who demanded the construction of a 'people's car' for its propaganda value. Next on the scene were the British, headed on site by a watchmaker with no specific orders other than to take control of a factory vacated by the Nazis. Cars were built, albeit rather badly and in decreasing numbers, before an autocratic and out of work German truck-builder was appointed to take over.

This man becomes the hero of our story, as he had a wider goal than simply building cars. He wished to restore Germany's standing in the world and the only way he knew how was to build and export VWs across the world. By 1965, he was selling over a million cars of a single design annually and had tentacles in close on 150 markets worldwide. Initially he restricted his ambition to getting the Beetle right, but by the mid-1950s he had sanctioned a 'sports' car under the general brand name. By the 1960s he had turned his attention to a wider range. By 1967 our hero's health declined and, as he was already well past retirement age, a successor was sought. Following his death in April 1968, came an even larger family saloon launched some months later.

Richard Copping   Kirkby Lonsdale, July 2004

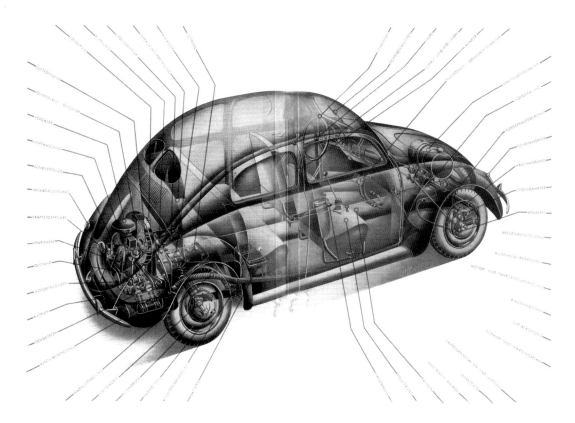

DER 'STRENGTH THROUGH JOY' WAGEN

With the accession of Adolf Hitler as Germany's Chancellor in January 1933, the first seed was sown for what would become the mighty Volkswagen Empire. That Hitler held a genuine fascination for the automobile cannot be denied, despite the fact that he never learned to drive. That his goal wasn't merely altruistic was inevitable. Hitler soon started to make speeches covering the issue of transport for the masses, which naturally sent his minions scuttling to fulfil his demands.

One such speech serves as well as any other to illustrate the massive propaganda value of his intentions, as he declared:-

"As long as the automobile stays the prerogative of the upper class, there remains a bitter feeling knowing that millions of brave, hardworking and able people will be excluded from the use of such a means of transport, something that would not only be useful to them with their kind of lifestyle, but which also would provide a source of pleasure on Sundays and Bank Holidays." On hearing such sentiments expressed, Ferdinand Porsche, the designer of several failed people's cars, was inspired once more.

Left: *The Nazi regime was responsible for production of more than just a 'sales brochure' to promote the people's car. This wonderfully detailed drawing of the KdF-Wagen acts as an index point for a detailed A-Z manual, which covered all aspects of the car's capabilities. Everything is explained in meticulous German detail, with many hints and tips, even down to including the best way to wash the car!*

He rushed back to his design studio to produce a strategy paper for a 'volksauto', a document that was guaranteed a future when presented to the Führer.

This is how the Beetle was born, but only through the recalcitrance of the Association of German Automakers (RDA) who, having been ordered to work with Porsche, refused to take the project seriously, no doubt in part thanks to the 'volksauto's' threat to their-own aspirations in such directions and via the Nazis wildly optimistic production calculations, is the massive and brand-new factory built near Fallersleben in the late-1930s explained. The all-enveloping propaganda machine that portrayed Hitler and his regime to the best effect leapt into action.

Top Right: *The Nazi sales brochure utilized colour for the cover and depicted a slightly stylised painting of the KdF-Wagen, plus a partially completed book of 'savings stamps'. A minimum saving limit was set of five-marks per week, althoug, if it was affordable extra payments could be made. Assuming the minimum amount was invested throughout, it would have taken the so-called 'saver' four-years and seven-months to pay the total required, which had finally been set at 1,190 marks, including compulsory insurance. Even then, a car could not be guaranteed. All the accumulated payments of completed stamp cards entitled someone to was eligibility for a car at some point in the future.*

Bottom Right: *Out and about went both prototype KdF-Wagens and a host of Nazi photographers to compile a series of life-style shots for use in a brochure designed to convince the German people that they too needed to join the savings scheme, one day becoming proud owners of a KdF-Wagen.*

Even at Hitler's demanded low selling price for the car of less than 1,000-marks, at a time when many workers brought home as little as 160-marks a month, some form of state aid savings scheme had to be devised. Over 336,000 workers signed up over the years and some 280-million marks were gathered into the Nazi's coffers.

The initial impetus of such a scheme, together with wildly optimistic production targets conjured up by the statisticians caused full-scale panic on the building front. Robert Ley, Head of the German Labour Front, confirmed that it was "the Führer's will that within a few years no less than 6,000,000 Volkswagens will be on German roads. In 10-years time there will be no working person in Germany who does not own a 'people's car'."

Without delay, some 15,000 acres were seized to build a vast mile-long factory. Hitler attended the foundation stone laying ceremony and promptly named both the plant and the car after one of the movements his subordinates used to indoctrinate the nation. The car became the 'Strength-through-Joy', or KdF-Wagen, while the factory and proposed town to surround it were similarly afflicted.

With war looming, Porsche, who was continually at the beck and call of his Nazi employers, had to turn his attention to the military applications of his beloved people's car and in so-doing produced both the highly versatile Kübelwagen, literally bucket car, the German equivalent to the US Jeep, and its amphibious partner, the even more ingenious Schwimmwagen.

Yet, KdF-Wagen production literally ground to a halt before it had even got into first gear, with fewer than 1,500 being built during the war. Many of these were in military guise, for example the Type 82E, a version that utilised the Kübel chassis to give greater ground clearance. The Nazis only saving grace was that the savers' money remained intact until it was seized by marauding Soviets. So much for the old fallacy that the KdF savers' were hoodwinked into contributing to Hitler's war machine!

SAVED BY THE BRITISH

Liberated by US forces in early April 1945, the factory built to produce the KdF-Wagen was in a sorry state. As the war progressed the vast plant had been used increasingly by the German Ministry of Armaments. Significantly, about half the total number of V1s or 'flying bombs', were produced there, making it an important target for allied bombing campaigns. The first of four major attacks came in the summer of 1943.

In May 1945, when British forces began to take control at Fallersleben they found that close to 60% of the factory was damaged to some extent, whilst just over 20% of the floor area was totally destroyed. Crucially, a Nazi decision to relocate vital equipment to the Belgium and Luxembourg border had been recinded thanks to US troop advances. If this relocation had occurred, any thought of re-starting production of any sort, would have probably been out of the question.

A Yorkshireman, Major Ivan Hirst was the 'Allies' senior resident officer at the ownerless KdF factory from his arrival in the early autumn of 1945. He was given no specific orders other than to 'take control'.

The German armaments industry was to be totally dismantled, with all the countries who had been at war with the Nazis able to bid for machines and tools as 'war reparations'. Those in charge accepted that the KdF factory had been genuinely built for the production of civilian cars and as such was not designated as a war plant destined for demolition. However, since it was not in operation in 1938 it fell foul of the ceiling set for the level of post-war German industry. Therefore, allegedly surplus to requirements, the KdF plant was deemed available for reparations. Complicated, or what?

An amazing, if not totally unexpected, lack of transport for occupying personnel saved the factory that had now assumed the eminently British name of the 'Wolfsburg Motor Works'. Hirst could go more than a little way to satisfy this pressing need by turning his attention to the wartime Kübelwagen. However, there was a technical hitch.

Way back in 1938, Ferdinand Porsche had visited the Budd Corporation in America, where he had acquired the rights to make the all-steel body for the KdF-Wagen using Budd techniques under licence. The deal was that if the Volkswagenwerk produced a variant of the saloon, assumed at the time to be a Cabrio, the American owned Ambi Budd of Berlin were to make the bodies. As a result of this, Kübelwagen bodies, in reality the second VW, had been built not at the KdF plant, but in Berlin.

At the end of the war not only was the Ambi Budd factory so badly damaged that most of the Kübel dies had been destroyed, but also what was left of the premises was now situated in the uncooperative Soviet sector. This catalogue of events led Hirst to seek approval to build the saloon.

Under the most difficult of circumstances, the British turned out no less than 1,785 Volkswagens during 1945. The following year they managed a staggering 10,020, followed by 8,987 cars in 1947. By a cruel twist of fate, it was the British who ironically saved Hitler's factory and thereby not only restored his dream but turned it into reality.

Inset: Major Ivan Hirst pictured in 1999, over 50-years after his period in charge at Wolfsburg. His kind words inspired many a budding author, while his recollections of the days of British rule at the VW factory remained crystal sharp to the end of his life in March 2000. A raconteur extraordinaire, when Hirst could be persuaded to address an invited audience he held them spellbound, while a great deal of theatrical business with his ever-present pipe ensured that the punch-line of a particular recollection was delivered with maximum effect. A short extract from a letter he attached to an article submitted for his scrutiny reveals how he was ever anxious to stress the 'team effort' of any British success. Referring to a fellow officer he wrote: "The important point about McEvoy is that he was the man that had the bright idea to use the VW for the occupation requirements – without his 'brain-wave, VWW would have quickly been eliminated."

Clearly, once it had been proved that car production at the Volkswagen factory was viable and the threat of reparations, or any other activity that would jeopardise the plants prospects, had more or less evaporated, the long-term future management structure had to be clarified. The solution came in the appointment of a former Opel Director. Born in January 1899, Heinz Nordhoff chose mechanical engineering as his field of study eventually joining BMW in 1927 before graduating to Opel.

After Opel became part of the American giant, General Motors, empire Nordoff quickly ascended the greasy pole, landing a directorship of Adam Opel AG in 1936. As the war progressed he was put in charge of the enormous Opel truck factory at Brandenburg. Sadly, for reasons out of his control, this move was almost his personal undoing. Output was naturally directed towards the military and for his dedicated service the Nazis presented Nordhoff with the equivalent of the British Empire Medal.

When the Americans took over the sector containing Brandenburg, they felt that the former director was tainted with the brush of Nazism and thus was unemployable. If the Americans had relented, or if Nordhoff had been deployed elsewhere in GMs vast empire during the war, there might well have been no Volkswagen. Yet another strange quirk of fate in the story

The convoluted way in which Nordhoff was interviewed for the post of deputy to Hermann Munch, an industrial lawyer, appointed as trustee in the absence of an official owner, but 'landed' the top job is more or less irrelevant to this story. The crucial point was that Nordhoff, working as a service supervisor for an old friend's widow, still hoped to get back to Opel.

He had little empathy for the Volkswagen, describing the car as "anything but a beauty" and "tarred with the brush of political trickery." If a letter from the US Military Government hadn't arrived at the crucial point declaring that former executives would never, ever work in the American Zone, Nordhoff simply wouldn't have taken the VW job, whatever the offer. As it was Nordhoff accepted, his only condition being that he wanted no interference, particularly from the British!

That the VW organisation became what it did (both so quickly and efficiently), is due to Nordhoff more than any other player in the story. Chance no longer played a part. Rather than chant by rote the landmarks in VWs blossoming fortunes, it is better to understand Mr Volkswagen's philosophy and let his own words, spoken all those years ago, explain why. The "small, cheap thing" with "more defects than a dog has fleas" was to be transformed.

Additionally though, it must not be forgotten that Nordhoff was a workaholic; from his days at Opel when he spent his 'holidays' on the shop floor to appreciate all the issues foremost on the minds of the assembly line workers, to his first six-months at VW, when he slept in a small room adjacent to his office, leaving friends and family to their own devices.

Most if not all of the key developments in the story were handled personally by Heinz Nordhoff, from product development to the crucial building of both minor and very major outposts right across the world. Nordhoff's initial messages were tough ones. He told his workers in 1948 that "it still takes us 400-hours to build a car. If we go on like this, we won't be going on much longer. We have to get it down to 100-hours per vehicle." Later he reflected that his only option had been to "start from scratch in the real sense of the word. 7,000 workers were painfully producing 6,000 cars a year, providing it did not rain too much."

As for his single solitary product, Nordhoff summarised with the less than complimentary phrases that it "really was what you call an ugly duckling", still "full of bugs." "There was so much to be done", as Nordhoff recalled in 1958. "Weak points in the design had to be ironed out, bottlenecks in production had to be broken, problems of material procurement, quality control, personnel had to be solved. There was no sales organisation … and I was determined that, of all things, Volkswagen should have the best service in the world." "Most of all", he added, "I wanted to obtain better-quality materials to put inside the car, specifically the engine, so as to keep it from breaking down so early."

Nordhoff's strategy for success was more or less unique in the automotive world. "I brushed away all of the temptations to change model and design. In any sound design there are almost unlimited possibilities; and this certainly was a sound one. I see no sense in starting anew every few years with the same teething troubles, making obsolete almost all the past. I went out on a limb. I took the chance of breaking away from the beaten path and of doing something unusual but highly constructive for transport hungry Europe, and not Europe alone."

"Offering people an honest value, a product of the highest quality, with low original cost and incomparable re-sale value, appealed more to me than being driven around by a bunch of hysterical stylists trying to sell people something they really do not want to have. Improving quality and value steadily, without increasing price … simplifying and intensifying service and spare parts systems, building a product of which I and every other Volkswagen worker can be truly proud and at the same time earning enough profit … to improve production facilities with the most modern equipment … and thus increase productivity and production every year: these things are … an engineers task."

"I am firmly convinced that there will always be a market in this world … for simple, economical and dependable transportation and for an honest value in performance and quality", Nordhoff declared. "I am convinced that, all over the world … there are millions of people who will gladly exchange chromium-plated gadgets and excessive power for economy, long life and inexpensive maintenance."

As the 1950s unfurled, flowered and finally faded as another decade dawned, Nordhoff's biggest problem was repeatedly one of sales outstripping supply.

Top Left: *Heinz Nordhoff – Director General, January 1st 1948 – 12th April 1968. Showered with honours during his lifetime, it was the undying loyalty of 'his' people and their total faith in him that mattered most to Nordhoff. On his death, official mourning was declared both at Wolfsburg and VW's Brazilian headquarters and a minute's silence was held in every VW plant. At Wolfsburg 45,000 workers and residents filed by his coffin, which lay in one of the factory halls. Countless thousands of people lined the streets on the day of his funeral to pay their last respects. Nordhoff's coffin was borne on a specially modified Transporter.*

Middle Left: *Very few KdF-Wagens survive. This one, dating from 1943, was ordered by the 'Chancellor's Office' and as such clearly was never intended for use by a member of the public.*

Bottom Left: *The Beetle – the product Nordhoff inherited, came to love and turn into a world-beater. This Deluxe example dates from the 1956 model year, a point when total Beetle sales had just turned the one million mark. Total production in the calendar year 1956 would amount to 333,190 cars. By 1968 this had shot up to 1,136,143 Beetles being produced annually.*

While his marketing men revelled in translating the phrase 'Es lohnt sich, auf einen Volkswagen zu warten' (a Volkswagen is worth waiting for) into every conceivable language imaginable, the Director General ploughed more and more money back into the organisation. Speaking in 1960, Nordhoff revealed that in the previous year 'we invested 500 million D-marks and in January boosted production by 100 VWs per day. In February, by another 100 per day and in March, once again by 100 per day. By the end of 1960 we shall produce 4,000 Volkswagens daily. Then we believe we shall have reached a balance between supply and demand, so that we can finally deliver Volkswagens to customers without a waiting period." Reality proved a little different, as the projected sales figures of 817,000 cars was in fact 38,000 fewer than reality

In 1961, Nordhoff presented a flower-bedecked Beetle to the International Red Cross. The occasion heralded the production of the 5-millionth such car since the end of the war and gave Nordhoff another opportunity to reveal his overriding priority, as well as a chance to reiterate aspects of his 'correctly set goal'.

The target was 'to develop one model of car to its highest technical excellence … the attainment of the highest quality …' destruction of the "notion that such high quality can only be attained at high prices" and to "give the car the highest value and to build it so that it retains that value …"

While many even today think of Volkswagen in the Nordhoff era simply as a machine to churn out Beetles, the Director General only put a halt to other products if he believed them superfluous to the organisation's immediate needs, when demand for the Beetle simply couldn't be met.

Volkswagen's next model, the Transporter was launched in 1950 and the unique position it held had to be supported in very much the same way as that of the Beetle. Like the saloon, demand soon came to outstrip supply. By 1954, 40,000 Transporters were being produced, although the daily capacity of 170 vehicles was only half the number of what could really have been sold. To help solve the problem a second factory, based at Hanover was commissioned, the first Transporters emerging from it in 1956.

Addressing a meeting of Transporter salesmen at the start of 1960, Nordhoff remarked that "the really big period for the Transporter hasn't even arrived yet. I have asked our sales department for years whether we shouldn't enlarge Hanover's capacity. I know that I have been tiresome about this, but I now ask with increasing urgency … Today we produce 530 a day and I am certain that even this isn't enough …"

As the third VW, the 'sporty' Karmann Ghia could rightly be described as a farmed-out product, it was only when the 1960s began to unfold that Nordhoff could finally turn his attention to truly additional products to capture other segments particularly of the home market. The launch of the VW 1500, the larger family-orientated saloon in September 1961 was once described as 'icing on the cake' by VW and in all probability such a sentiment was shared by Nordhoff. His philosophy and the strategy he brought to Volkswagen in 1948 became clear very quickly and by the 1960s had been well and truly achieved. Now he was able to widen Volkswagen's stage!

Top Right: *The Transporter, seen here in luxury Deluxe Microbus form, was a Nordhoff product through and through, whatever arguments might be put forward. During 1950, the year of its official launch, 8,059 Transporters took the world by storm. September 1956 saw the 200,000th, while August 1959 heralded the first half million, but that figure had doubled again when the millionth Transporter arrived in September 1962. The peak was reached in 1964, when 200,235 vans were produced.*

Middle Right: *The Karmann Ghia as launched in 1955. Nordhoff had been ultra-cautious in sanctioning the addition of a 'sports' saloon to the range, albeit that the majority of the work lay with the coachbuilders, Wilhelm Karmann. Conscious that Wolfsburg could not keep up with demand for the Beetle, he was naturally reluctant to divert resources to any other project. Fortuitously, the KG sold well, only finally being withdrawn from the range when new water-cooled Volkswagens emerged.*

Bottom Right: *The VW 1500, seen here in 1500S guise, only appeared once Nordhoff had finally caught up with the demand for Beetles. Some writers persist in repeating the fallacy that the car was introduced as a replacement for the Beetle, but in reality the Type Three range was VW's idea of a larger family saloon that the Type One owner might aspire to.*

Nordhoff was patriotic to his home country and felt passionately that Germany should play a prominent part in the world. The philosophy and strategy that he brought to Volkswagen in 1948 soon became clear. In 1951, he spoke of his ambition saying, "I regard it as my life's aim to build this factory into Europe's premier car plant."

Three-years earlier the same blunt message had been even more forcefully expressed when Nordhoff addressed his troops. "For the first time in its history the Volkswagenwerk will this year, have to face the necessity of standing on its own feet. It is up to us to make this largest of all German motor car factories a decisive factor for Germany's peacetime economy."

Awarded Honorary Citizenship of Wolfsburg when the millionth Beetle made its debut, the citation confirmed appreciation of Nordhoff's stance. "To the pioneer of Germany's reconstruction, whose efforts as employer ensured that from an almost hopeless situation the Volkswagen became within a few years a world-wide success …"

A recognised authority, K B Hopfinger, wrote in 1956 that Nordhoff's achievement was "linked" with West Germany's recovery, while the man himself was able to say that the millionth celebrations had "provided a glimpse of the world which Volkswagen has conquered."

Nordhoff knew that he had achieved what the Nazis had failed dismally to do; he had conquered the world. By 1966, just two years before his death, Nordhoff had seen seven million Volkswagens exported and in excess of 500,000 manufactured in countries other than Germany. Export sales in 1965 to the USA alone amounted to some 5,600,000DM, while in Brazil every second car sold there was a VW. The marketing men, never ones to miss an opportunity, had plastered their brochures with the message "Why is the Volkswagen a favourite in 136 countries?"

Below: *The US market was crucial to global expansion. US Beetle's soon became identifiable by oddities such as bullet style indicators and additional legislation appeasing bumpers.*

FIT TO FACE THE WORLD

When Ferdinand Porsche presented his proposals for a 'volksauto' to the Nazis in early 1934, he was establishing the general principles for the post-war Beetle, which would remain in continuous production until the summer of 2003. Porsche declared that his car would be an everyday vehicle of normal dimensions, but of lightweight construction. A realistic top speed, comparable to other cars of the age and an ability to climb, were additional primary considerations, as was a decent sized, comfortable interior, while its make-up was to be such that servicing would be minimal. Porsche wrote of a 26bhp engine, capable of achieving 100kph and of a projected selling price of 1550 RM.

Numerous prototypes were put through their paces, while Hitler and his henchmen remained resolute on the all-important issue of price. Porsche found this neigh on impossible to work with, but the KdF-Wagen emerged to be present at the corner-stone laying ceremony of the factory to be built especially for its production. By 1938, the engine was finalised as a flat-four air-cooled unit, with a capacity of 985cc, which developed 23bhp and offered a maximum and cruising speed of 100km/h (60mph).

Above: *Although not strictly relevant to the story told here, the wartime version of the Beetle, the Kübel-Wagen, helped to ensure that the post-war car would have a little more power than the pre-hostility KdF prototypes.*

With the engine positioned at the rear, the essential control cables passed through a central backbone on a lightweight chassis, made up of two ribbed floor-pans welded to the aforementioned central tunnel. Suspension was of Porsche's own patent: transverse torsion bars at both front and rear, with trailing arms at the former and a swing axle at the back. The brakes were cable-operated drums, while the electrics were six-volt, with the battery away from dampness, positioned somewhat inaccessibly under the rear seat.

Porsche's team smoothed and refined the original unusual body, retaining its separate front and rear wing panels. They had added two small rear windows, a pair of bumpers and altered the doors to hinge at the front rather than the previous 'suicide' approach. Running boards made the vehicle look more complete, while transforming the boot lid into a single sheet of metal, rather than the previous knuckle scraping two-part arrangement, made it easier to remove the spare wheel.

The Beetle 1945 to 1949

Only one change of any significance had occurred during the war years to Porsche's final pre-production KdF-Wagen, when almost by accident the saloon acquired the upgraded power unit designed to make the Kübelwagen better equipped to carry out its appointed tasks. Achieved by boring out the cylinders, the 'new' 1131cc engine developed a considerably more powerful 25bhp. Under different circumstances, mass production should have been a realistic objective. Instead, that the earliest post-war Beetles were built at all has to be attributed to British ingenuity, as supplies of materials including steel, glass, batteries, upholstery fabric, tyres and even electrical components were at best spasmodic, or at worst non-existent. Former suppliers premises were either devastated by bomb damage, or not located in the accessible western sector. Realistically, it was only because Volkswagen was operated by and working for the Allies that it received anything at all!

Above: *While the Deluxe or Export version of the Beetle wasn't launched until July 1949, attempts were made to upgrade the car's specification before then. Invariably these centred on chromed bumpers, headlamp rims and hubcaps, while paintwork tended to be glossier and upholstery less akin to army blankets! The car shown is something of an anomaly in that it demonstrates all the hallmarks of such attempts, but was produced in June 1949 when the Export model was only weeks away. Perhaps all is explained as it was destined for Brussels and not for domestic consumption.*

For a time roof pressings were made of two sheets of steel welded together as large enough singles were not available, which resulted in an ugly and leaky lap joint. Stocks of carburettors, made under licence by Pierburg in Berlin to a French Solex-design, soon became dangerously short. Hirst dismantled one of the remaining ones building two piles on his desk.

12

One could be manufactured in the factory; the other was sub-contracted to a Brunswick camera firm, well used to making small precision parts in brass. Hirst later scotched rumours that army blankets were used to upholster seat frames!

Poor paintwork resulted in rusty Beetles within 12-months of assembly, while engines, thanks to the inferior parts used, were unreliable. Hirst's recollection of 'damaged nylons' was the most unusual. Cardboard was used to insulate the battery terminals from the steel protective cover. The cardboard rotted away when exposed to acid fumes. Should the positive terminal and the cover come into contact, the spring holding everything in place became hot, acting like the element of an electric fire.

Hirst resolved occurring problems but also tried to develop quality standards. Improvements in the manufacturing process led to a reduction in transmission noise, the problem of fast wearing suspension components was removed by better quality control, while the engine's cylinder life was lengthened by improving the finish of interior surfaces. However, a harsh winter and a lack of fuel were sufficient to bring production to a halt.

By the time Nordhoff was appointed, a few cars were benefiting from a smattering of chrome and more glossy paint in an ad hoc attempt to generate exports. Nevertheless, Nordhoff knew that, if the Beetle was to be the world-beater he desired, a planned strategy had to be adopted and fast.

Top Right: *That the car photographed dates from 1950, a year after the period described in the accompanying text is irrelevant, for this is a Standard model, a time-warp vehicle virtually identical to the cars manufactured by the British. Distinguishing features of such cars, apart from the obvious split-rear-screen, include the absence of trim and chrome, plus delicate grooved bumpers, large wheels and near non-existent rear lights.*

Middle Right: *Throughout the 1950s, VW relied on the work of the illustrator Bernd Reuters to promote their products. He elongated and streamlined each vehicle's look, making it appear stylish and sophisticated, without losing the essential features of the original. The same drawing could well be used on several occasions over the years ahead, although invariably re-coloured and with details amended as VW updated its product.*

Bottom Right: *The Beetle was completely re-vamped in October 1952. The main features included a new design for the dashboard, additional trim inset into the rubbers around the car's windows, simpler (more sturdy looking) bumpers and re-designed tail-lights. Although Britain wasn't an official VW market at this point in time, some right-hand-drive examples of the 'split window' Beetle do exist, having been either exported to South Africa, or even assembled there from the parts provided by Wolfsburg. The clearly visible folding sunroof first appeared on the Beetle on 28th April 1950 and cost an extra 250DM.*

Do you like the European look in automobiles? Are you fond of clean-cut stream lines? Do you like to ride in easy comfort, yet would like to have a means of transportation that is downright cheap to operate? If such is the case, the Volkswagen, the leading European car in its field, is exactly what you are looking for. Technicians the world over say that the Volkswagen is the most sensible automobile ever built and that it is years ahead in design. The Volkswagen was designed by a genius as unique in his field as Caruso was as a tenor. The Volkswagen Sedan is built in two models, Standard and De Luxe. Both models are handsome in their shining metallic finish. The De Luxe Sedan offers a choice of bewitching colors. Expensive upholstery and handsome practical fittings blend into a harmonious whole with typical European discretion. All Volkswagen models offer the same basic features that make Volkswagens so outstanding. All have that surprisingly fast get away, that smooth and safe driving thanks to marvelous suspension and a low center of gravity, and that extraordinary economy of operation combined with great driving comfort which characterize the Volkswagen and make it unequalled in its field.

13

The Deluxe or 'Export' Model

The Export, or Deluxe, Beetle launched in July 1949 was realistically little more than an exercise in upgrading the car's aesthetics, but the result was an immediate increase in sales! Externally the new model had a wider offering of more attractive paint shades, plus high quality bright-work adorning the waistline, bonnet and running boards. It saw the first appearance of the famous V over W roundel on the car's bonnet, and redesigned sturdier looking over-riders, while other details abounded. The externally-mounted horn of old was carefully concealed behind the front-left wing, while dainty, apparently decorative, grilles adorned both. Chrome hubcaps of a standard design became the norm.

The inside of the car set a new standard in good taste. Utilitarian black Bakelite was replaced by an upmarket shade of ivory, which extended to such items as a new two-spoke steering wheel, the gear lever and all operational knobs. A clock, or radio, complimented the single instrument gauge, with a speed indicator that (to modern eyes at least) seemed to operate backwards! The front seats were redesigned so that they became adjustable for both rake and forward movement, replacing the previous and eminently primitive arrangement of wing nuts. Cloth grab handles were added to assist rear seat passengers, while a couple of bolster cushions were thought by most to be an unnecessary extra. A full cloth headlining replaced the acres of condensation-inducing bare painted metal, which had been the norm since day one.

Possibly what really made the Export model stand out, in what had been a grey and austere post war world, was a sensitive and attractive use of carefully colour-matched materials. Exterior paint colours were subtly toned to both carpets and headliners, with a reasonable number of options being employed as a result.

From a production total of just 19,244 cars in 1948, the figure escalated to over 46,000 in 1949, while in 1950, the first complete year for the Export model, there was a further significant increase to just short of 82,000 cars. The great Beetle advance had begun, with cars popping up in countries like Belgium, Denmark, Luxembourg, Sweden, and Switzerland, each of course appropriately backed by full service and after sales facilities.

Top Left: *This 1956-model car painted in Reed Green has been owned by the same family for all but five years of its lengthy life. Like many others. the keeper decided to replace the antiquated semaphores with flashing indicators.*

Bottom Left: *From April 1951 to August 1959, when it was simplified, this beautifully crafted badge adorned the bonnet of all Deluxe model Beetles. It depicts an adaptation of the coat of arms of the one-time owner of Castle Wolfsburg, whose land was requisitioned to build the Volkswagen factory. The famous V over W symbol was designed in the 1930s by engine designer, Reimspiess, a member of Porsche's team.*

The 1950s

The Beetle's convolvulus like grip on the world started in earnest with the dawning of the new decade. March 1950 saw the 100,000-post-war car roll off the assembly line, while production of VWs started in Southern Ireland from what were known as CKD kits. This (CKD) stood for Completely Knocked Down; in other words Wolfsburg made all the bits and exported a 'kit' to the satellite, which in turn 'glued' them together.

South Africa became the first dedicated satellite, commencing 'manufacturing' operations in August 1951, while by the end of October of the same year; total Beetle numbers had hit the quarter million mark. During 1951, a total of 35,742 cars had been exported to 29 eager countries. By 1952, over 41% of Beetles built were destined for the export market.

Throughout the 1950s, the Beetle evolved both mechanically and bodily, while sales soared to astronomic proportions as market after market fell for what was now an obvious appeal and reputation for reliability and longevity. Hydraulic brakes replaced cables in mid-1950, while from October 1952 synchromesh appeared as if by magic on all forward gears with the exception of first. The same month was significant in other ways, as the Beetle received its first serious makeover since the launch of the Export model.

Bright work mushroomed, while the bumpers became sturdier if less attractive. By then the traditional skinny 16" wheels were discarded in favour of 15" ones, which in turn sported slightly heftier 5.60-15 tyres. Inside, the dash was totally re-designed, the open glove compartments of old being replaced by a single lidded one, whilst a carefully designed radio speaker grille dominated the overall layout. Another 'gold-star' to the stylists!

In March 1953 the Beetle lost its distinctive split rear screen, replaced as it was by a single oval shaped pane. The 23% increase in glass size did more for the Beetle than most of the far more significant changes already outlined and a trade quickly built up in hacking out the metal between the two panes of glass on older cars.

Top Right: *Whereas Reuters had previously concentrated virtually all his efforts on the frontal appearance of the Beetle, with the vast increase in the size of the rear-window it was all change. Not only did the rear end appear frequently on the internal pages, brochures were also produced showing the car at such an angle on the cover, as is the case with the cropped image depicted here. In a nice touch to promote the 'acres' of glass on show, the rear passenger is drawn turning towards 'camera'. Such was VWs conviction in their product that the brochure cover lacked any form of text!*

Bottom Right: *The Beetle circa August 1957 and onwards: this particular first-year example is finished in Diamond Grey, which is in reality more of a light metalic gold.*

March 1953 was significant for another reason, as this month saw the formation of VW do Brazil, with an initial purpose of assembling CKD Beetles. The operation flourished, eventually becoming the most significant non-German VW operation, producing a whole range of unique models as well as both the Fusca, the name by which the Beetle became known, and the ubiquitous Transporter. Brazil exported vehicles as well, particularly to African satellites: was there no end to their talents?

While most people were thinking of yuletide festivities in the same year, Volkswagen was busy introducing a new, more powerful, engine for their premier product. 1131cc became 1192cc and 25bhp leapt up to 30bhp, achieved by altering the size of the bore and fitting larger inlet valves. August 1955 was significant in a number of ways. Not only did post war production figures achieve the magic million amidst unparalleled and lengthy celebrations, but also VW revamped their package once more, the most notable visible change being the appearance of twin exhaust pipes. From this point, model and calendar years became different, with production of the following year's Beetle commencing immediately after the factory's annual holiday, which took place at the end of July. Confusing undoubtedly and so to clarify, the first time the new 1956 year model appeared was in August 1955.

Above: *Thanks to Nordhoff's policy of continuous improvement through gradual change, the task of identifying Beetle models is not easy. Here is a 1962 Deluxe, which could be mistaken for the car pictured at the bottom of page 15. Telltale signs of a later car are neat teardrop-shaped indicators perched on the front wing tops and a simplified bonnet badge. Not visible, are three-section and larger tail-light housings, while hidden in the engine compartment is the 34bhp block, quieter and more powerful thanks to a slower fan speed and an increased compression ratio.*

It was during 1955, that cars bound for the USA began to take on a distinctive appearance of their own. Exports had initially been extremely slow and despite a contract signed with Max Hoffmann, a successful and well-known New York importer of high-powered cars, progressed little further. At the end of 1953 Nordhoff decided the only course was to create a sales network under the control of the Volkswagenwerk itself. Thanks to the ability of Gottfried Lange and the enthusiasm of Will Van de Kamp, a former Messerschmidt pilot who spoke little English, the foundations of a dealer network were established and 6,343 Beetles were sold in 1954. This figure jumped to 32,662 the following year, while Nordhoff tied up the loose ends via a new corporation, 'Volkswagen of America'.

The quirks of both national and state legislation and the whims of potential owners in the USA had to be catered for by Nordhoff's advancing army! So, out went the primitive semaphores to be replaced by a unique bullet shaped indicator, which was positioned close to the car's headlamps. Sealed beam headlamps became the norm, as did two-tier bumpers, useful in a country where the homespun product tended to feature brash chrome bumpers that sat higher off the ground than the German product. Still known by enthusiasts as 'towel-rails' to this day, the new bumpers proved so popular that they became an official option for most markets within a very short space of time.

February 1956 heralded the departure from Wolfsburg of the 500,000th Volkswagen for export, while 11-months later the 100,000th Beetle destined for Sweden bid farewell to the mother plant. Some sort of significant figure materialised virtually every month; a press release writer's dream! Fast forward to August 1957 for yet another drastic update of the cars specification as the oval rear window was to be replaced by a rectangular offering.

This was some 95% larger than its predecessor and was a much welcomed addition. The size of the front screen was also increased at the same time, although by a mere 17%, while the car's interior once again benefited from an entirely new dashboard. Amazingly, this latest design would survive, albeit in a slightly simpler form, to the demise of the Beetle over 45-years later, suggesting that the balance between glovebox and speaker, single dial and radio blanking panel, ashtray and control positions was more or less perfect. At the end of 1957 Volkswagen (Australasia) was formed in Melbourne. In the same month (December), the two-millionth Beetle was built; while the demand continued and just over 18-months later (by August 1959) another million had been added to the total.

Below: *This picture features a Beetle of 1965 vintage. The easy way to spot the difference between this and earlier models is to glance at the size of the side windows, which are larger. To achieve this, Nordhoff's designers slimmed down the pillars.*

The 1960s

In June 1960, the 500,000th Beetle destined for the USA set sail, just weeks before the new model year saw the car upgraded once more. The trusty but now slightly underpowered 30bhp engine was replaced on all but the standard model with a more powerful unit, which had been 'road tested' in the Transporter since May 1959.

The 'new' engine boasted 34bhp, the compression ratio having been raised from 6.6:1 to 7.0:1, while the crankshaft had become stronger. No doubt to the amazement of many car enthusiasts, this engine was still available when the last German Beetles were built in 1978 and lingered on throughout the 1980s at Puebla, VW de Mexico's stronghold.

While there was a number of other changes made; to note two should be sufficient to demonstrate Nordhoff's policy of continually improving the product. The gearbox became an all-synchromesh affair, and at long last VW abandoned the semaphore in every market. True to form, the 'old' rear housing was used for the new combined functions of indicator, tail and brake lights, while on the front wings top-mounted, elegant, chromed, 'tear-drop' shaped indicators appeared.

Above: *The 1500 Beetle, introduced in August 1966, was the first to feature disc brakes, although these were not included on US specification cars. The engine lid was re-designed to make the license plate sit more vertically and a 1500 'badge' was added.*

The 1962 model saw the first emergence of a fuel gauge, a feature that came as a great relief to those panicky owners who were previously reliant on a reserve gallon of 'juice', which was released by the flick of a 'tap' when the car began to cough and splutter. By 1964 the long-standing fabric sunroof was being replaced by a smaller wind-back affair in metal, while in 1965 all the windows were increased in size once more, making the Beetle look far more modern.

For the 1966 model year, along came a 1300 engine sporting 40bhp, which had been introduced as part of Nordhoff's grand scheme for keeping pace with the ever-proliferating numbers of other small car designs beginning to emerge both at home and abroad, including Japan. The 0-60 acceleration time reduced to 25secs while the top and cruising speed increased from 71mph to 76. Most importantly, the car appeared considerably less pedestrian in performance.

Having accepted that bigger engines had to be the way forward for the Beetle if it was to stay ahead of the competition, Nordhoff shocked the purists just 12-months later by adding a further larger engine to the range, while retaining both the 1300 and the old 1200 unit in production. The Beetle was becoming a multi-faceted product! The 1493cc unit produced a very useful 44bhp. Such was the power of this vehicle; that for the first time the Beetle was fitted with disc brakes up-front, although in true VW style the cars that were built for the United States market didn't match the rest. Instead Americans were offered 12-volt electrics and vertically positioned headlamps, which in turn necessitated a re-design for the front wings, or should we say fenders.

The 1967 6-volt 1500 Beetle has gone down in history as one of the finest of VW's offerings. Retaining, as it did, most of the aesthetically pleasing aspects of the Beetle of old, but at the same time becoming a real driver's car, surviving examples command a premium price when compared to their more humble brethren.

Most enthusiasts think of the Beetle's golden age coming to an abrupt halt with Nordhoff's death in April 1968, while many see the 'New Beetle', introduced in August 1967 for the 1968 model year, as the beginning of a slippery slope into unacceptable practices! Few however, take the trouble to check the dates and realise that the transformed car that the marketing men could realistically describe as 'Die Neuen Käfer' emerged from Wolfsburg while Mr Volkswagen was still very much at the helm.

Capturing some of the features already bestowed on the US models described above, the Beetle's appearance was dramatically altered by new box, or 'u' section bumpers, which were positioned higher on the car than previously. This in turn demanded that both the luggage compartment and engine lids had to be shortened. Vertical headlamps and the necessity of redesigned wings, plus larger, chunkier rear light housings, really made a difference.

The near universal application of 12-volt electrics had to be significant for sales as it countered the only serious criticism the Beetle had to face. Fuelling the car without resorting to opening the luggage compartment lid made sense too! To satisfy US requests a semi-automatic version of the Beetle was also launched, with the flourish the Americans demanded.

The 1960s saw production records tumble; 200,000 Beetles had already been exported to the US by October 1962, while by November 1966, nine million Beetles had been built since the end of the war. In 1967, 8,400 Beetles rolled off the assembly line of the new, purpose-built, factory in Puebla, Mexico. This outpost would nurture Nordhoff's heritage for 35-years after his death.

Below: *Whilst this car dates from 1969 its outward appearance matches that of the variant launched as the 'New Beetle' for the 1968 model year. While aesthetically it might not be as appealing, it met the safety requirements demanded in the USA and it presented to the world a revitalised and more aggressive stance.*

The Volkswagen Transporters

THE 'BOX ON WHEELS'.

When German production of the first incarnation of the Transporter, the Type Two or in modern parlance, the 'Splittie' van, came to an end in July 1967, not far off 2-million examples had been built worldwide. Absolute peanuts in comparison to the Beetle of course, but nevertheless another phenomenal success story for Volkswagen, particularly when the pioneering nature of the vehicle's origins and the spawning of a whole new attitude to camping activities, are taken into consideration.

A few landmarks are worth noting as with the Beetle. The 100,000th Transporter left Wolfsburg on 9th October 1954, in a year when Volkswagen would build 40,199 such vehicles at a rate of around 153 per working day. The 200,000th Transporter followed just under two-years later, on 13th September 1956, but this time emerged from a purpose-built factory at Hanover, which had opened for business on 8th March of the same year.

Above: *When it came to illustrations for the sales brochures, Reuters's was just as adept at enhancing the Transporter's appearance. Many a photographer will crouch down in front of his subject to make it appear larger than it is in reality, which is what he has done with the vehicle on the right of the drawing shown here.*

The 500,000th barrier was broken on 25th August 1959 and the all-important millionth vehicle saw light of day on 2nd October 1962. From 1958 onwards in excess of 100,000 transporters were built every year, with the highest figure of all coming in 1964, when 187,947 vans were produced in Germany alone. When production ceased in July 1967 to make way for the new Transporter model, 1,833,000 Splitties had been built at either Wolfsburg or Hanover. The South African and Australian factories were responsible for a further 35,000, while in Brazil, where production lingered on until 1975 an additional 400,000 Transporters were constructed.

With Porsche pre-occupied first with the Beetle and latterly military vehicles until 1945, the Transporter can legitimately be described as the brain-child of three men, an extrovert Dutch entrepreneur Ben Pon, Ivan Hirst and Heinz Nordhoff. Following the disappearance from the Wolfsburg Motor Works of a useful heavy engineering unit and its attendant flotilla of forklifts, Hirst needed some sort of load carrier to transport Beetle parts from one assembly line to another.

Never one to be thwarted for long, Hirst sat and sketched out what became the 'Plattenwagen', a load carrier utilising an available Kübelwagen chassis. It was comprised of a flat bed, Beetle running gear and an open cab, placed directly above the engine at the rear of the vehicle. Useful in its own right at the factory for many years to come, the Plattenwagen gave would-be Beetle exporter, Ben Pon, a remarkable idea. However, realising the commercial potential of the Plattenwagen, Pon tried to secure an import licence, but the Dutch authorities refused his application, thanks primarily to an unacceptable driving position. As a result, on April 23rd 1947 Pon presented Ivan Hirst with a simple child-like sketch of something which bore a remarkable resemblance to what was to emerge from Wolfsburg less than three-years later, namely a box-shaped load carrying vehicle, with its engine placed directly over the rear axle and its driver perched over the front wheels.

Sadly, Hirst's boss, Colonel Charles Radclyffe, the head of engineering construction in the British zone, deemed Wolfsburg Motor Works to be stretched to capacity on the Beetle front and therefore unable to cope with a second product. However, the idea wasn't forgotten and when Nordhoff got 'behind the wheel' the aborted project was swiftly revived.

Top & Middle Right: *The pre-1955 van can be easily recognised by its lack of a 'peaked cap', a device added when the range was revised to aid interior ventilation and perhaps accidentally improve the vehicle's looks. In the first year of full production the basic panel van accounted for a little over 70% of the total. By 1955, due to both an increasing popularity of the other models, plus more available options, this figure had dropped to less than 40%. Over 100,000 Transporters were built before the peak-cap arrived on the scene.*

Bottom Right: *Note the prominent use of the VW emblem on this pre-1955 panel van! This logo was originally entwined with symbols of the Nazi regime, Ivan Hirst charged his design department to come up with something better, or to re-work it accordingly. The cogwheels of the Third Reich were removed, the letters reversed out and Hirst approved a 'logo' that is recognised worldwide. Perhaps a quick note should be made that the word Volkswagen is and always has been one. Why nobody questioned the use of the letter 'W' as well as the initial 'V' perhaps we shall never know.*

Nordhoff gave VW design chief, Alfred Haesner the go ahead in the autumn of 1948. He anticipated that it would not take long to prepare initial sketches and plans, as what was being asked for was little more than a box on wheels. On 20th November two designs were presented to Nordhoff; one with a straight and flat driver's cab, which he firmly rejected and a second, with a slightly raked front, that was given the go-ahead.

The Beatle's 25hp engine was positioned at the rear of the new vehicle, while the standard VW crash-box of the day was bolted directly to it. For the initial prototype, the 'box' body was bolted straight onto the Beetle chassis, complete with both torsion bars and running gear. The first vehicle was completed on 9th March 1949, with testing starting some three-weeks later on 5th April. Sadly, the Beetle's chassis was totally unsuited to its new task: it was simply not strong enough to withstand the increased stresses and, as a result it twisted and folded when weight was placed in the load carrying area.

Above: *This Transporter, dating from 1956, has been fitted with one of the numerous optional extras available, namely 'Safari windows' (M113). This van is finished in Dove Blue, as are the vans shown on the previous page. This colour was the one that was most commonly seen on the workhorse vans throughout the 17-year production run.*

Nordhoff, determined to go into production before the end of the year, set his design team to work once more, with the task of completing a brand new 'chassis' and revising the body within the tightest of schedules. The plan now revolved around a unitary design, with the body and floor welded together on a sub-frame consisting of two hefty longitudinal members welded together via two equally robust cross members.

The introduction of a reduction drive, an idea 'borrowed' from the wartime Kübelwagen, gave essential higher ground clearance and a wider transmission ratio.

22

The 'new' Transporter was rigorously tested over some 12,000 kilometres of the worst roads in Lower Saxony and proved itself more than tough enough to do the job. In turn this allowed a further four variations of prototype to be built, a panelvan, pickup, minibus and a vehicle suitable for use by the ambulance and post office.

Nordhoff launched his revolutionary Type Two Transporter; a vehicle, which like the Beetle, had no official name, to a fascinated press on 12th November 1949. He summarised it as, a "combination of a unitised body with the main characteristics of the Volkswagen." Capable of carrying 750kg, it weighed in at a mere 975kg and was eminently capable of 25mpg, so that on a single tank of fuel 500km could be covered. Crucially the Type 2 did not rely on preconceived ideas, outmoded traditions and existing tools and dies, a point the Director General was quick to capitalise on. "Our Transporter", he said will be "without compromises. This is why we did not start from the available chassis, but from the cargo space. This cargo space consists of the driver's seat at the front and the engine at the back. ... With this van and only this van, the cargo space lies directly between the axles. The driver sits in the front and there is equal weight in the back due to the fuel tank and engine; that is the best ..."

Nordhoff was also swift to condemn the accepted norm in commercial transport. "The famous cab above the engine gave such horrendous handling characteristics that we never even considered it", he said. "You can tell by looking at the state of the trees in the British Zone how well the British Army lorries, built on this principle, handle on wet roads when they are not loaded!"

The first production vehicles started to come off the assembly line in February 1950, destined for selected major customers for use as 'test' vehicles, and ready for a spectacular launch at the Geneva Motor Show in March 1950. 'Mass production', at a rate of ten Transporters per day, started on 10th March. The price of 5,850DM, compared to a Deluxe Beetle at 5,700DM was guaranteed to generate interest; the fact that there was little to compare it with virtually ensured its success. One modern day motoring journalist has described the 'average truck or van' of the 1940s or early 1950s "whether built in America or Europe" as "a noisy, uncomfortable, diesel-engined monster capable of little more than 40mph and with little in the way of stopping power." The VW was something different. Another author, writing little more than a decade after the Transporter's introduction, proclaimed that "Nordhoff blazed a trail", while all would concur that Britain's offering of a Morris J-Type and France's Citroen Type H were left far behind by the Volkswagen.

Top Right/Middle Bottom: *Reuters demonstrated the various more workaday applications of the Transporter with his customary skill. From the top to bottom there is the 'Delivery Van', the 'Pickup' and the 'multipurpose Kombi'. All are finished in the artist's representation of Dove Blue!*

The Volkswagen Delivery Van
The loading capacity is 170 cu. ft. or 1830 lbs. The large-sized rear door and wide double side doors combine to speed up loading and unloading

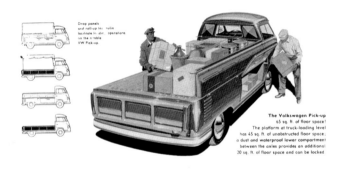

Drop panels and roll-up tailgate facilitate loading operations on the nimble VW Pick-up.

The Volkswagen Pick-up
65 sq. ft. of floor space! The platform at truck-loading level has 45 sq. ft. of unobstructed floor space; a dust and waterproof lower compartment between the axles provides an additional 20 sq. ft. of floor space and can be locked

The Volkswagen Kombi
The multipurpose Kombi is a truly versatile vehicle.

The Volkswagen Micro Bus

Developing the Product

Nordhoff's creed of continual model improvement extended to the Transporter. However, unlike the Beetle, where the choice was restricted to a standard model, Deluxe (with or without sunroof) and the niche market convertible, the Transporter came to be offered in a wide variety of different guises as the years went by.

One other consideration also needs a mention at this stage, namely the option of 'purchasing' a Transporter finished merely in primer. A brisk business sprang up, as firms personalised their purchases with company logos and house colours, so much so that sales brochures intriguingly referred to 'publicity space'. "Cost conscious businessmen have worked out that billboard space equal in size to the advertising area on the VW Delivery Van costs more in one year than the entire VW. That is why they are so anxious to utilise both panels and top for impressive publicity."

The basic Transporter, or Panelvan, made its official debut on 8th March 1950 and was followed in May by the Kombi and the Microbus. The first of June 1951 heralded the arrival of the many windowed, sunroof cosseted Deluxe Microbus, while on 13th December 1951 the Ambulance followed. The Single Cab Pickup made its debut on 25th August 1952, but it was over another six-years, 3rd November 1958 to be precise, before the Double Cab Pickup joined it. Last, but not least, Volkswagen added a High Roof Model to the range. To all but those strictly in the know, it should come as something of a surprise that no mention has been made of a camper van version of the Transporter, while one or two may be somewhat baffled by VW's official terminology for some of the derivations of their commercial vehicle.

The Panelvan should require little by way of explanation, other than to say that it was most often seen throughout its 17-year run in a shade known as 'Taubenblau', or Dove Blue. The Kombi on the other hand requires a word or two, as the world's first, albeit very basic, 'people carrier', long before such a term had even been invented! In reality, the Kombi was little more than a Panelvan with three side windows and removable seats in the 'load area'.

The Microbus had fixed seats and a better trim level, while the Deluxe Microbus was undoubtedly launched for the higher class market. Invariably referred to nowadays as the Samba, the Sondermodell (special model), or Deluxe Microbus, boasted four instead of three windows along each passenger section, eight dainty 'skylights' set into the roof, an executive wrap-around window at both rear corners and by the standard of the time, truly luxurious trim.

Top Middle & Bottom Left: *And so to the more upmarket applications and the VW ambulance! Why this vehicle was included in a good number of brochures is hard to imagine, as even the text does little more than claim it to be 'a special-purpose vehicle'. From the top, there is the Microbus, the Microbus Deluxe and finally, the ambulance.*

CABRIOLET

De mest kritiske automobilister er uden tvivl de, som kræver sportsbetonet kørsel i en helt åben vogn, samtidig med at de stiller store fordringer til såvel teknik som komfort. De ønsker et køretøj, som er absolut væsensforskelligt fra alle andre. For disse liebhavere har Volkswagenwerk løst proble-

met på en yderst tiltalende måde med VW-cabriolet. Lige-gyldigt hvor den ses, skaber den berettiget opmærksomhed og beundring. — Intet under at så mange damer med ud-præget god smag kører VW-cabriolet!

Above: *Throughout the Fifties little if any use was made of photography when VW sales brochure were compiled. Instead the undoubted talents of artist Ernst Reuters were employed. Without losing the overall look of the vehicle, he was able to make the product look both more streamlined and enticing. Often the same artwork was used over a number of years, subtly re-coloured and amended as the Beetle was continually updated. The Cabriolets in the main picture (above) can be dated to 1956 or 1957, thanks to the addition of twin exhaust pipes to an earlier drawing if nothing else. Note how Reuters has shown the wings with almost sports car like contours, while the seats look so luxurious that they might have been borrowed from the most expensive of cars. Every aspect is highly detailed, even down to the two green tinted see-through sun-visors and the large chrome plated ashtray in the rear passenger compartment.*

Right: *Cropped from the cover of a late Fifties brochure, here's the Sunroof Deluxe model, which has been given the full Reuters treatment. Note how the sunroof is more or less the full length of the roof, which of course it wasn't, while the clever positioning of the male passenger implies little or no intrusive metalwork down the side of the vehicle. The tyres have become chunkier than reality, the frontal appearance less 'bug-like', but the artwork is nevertheless totally believable.*

Above: *The Beetle sported an oval-shaped rear window for little over four-years, but this period, March 1953 to July 1957, more than any other epitomised both expansion in a worldwide market and a realisation that the Beetle was unrivalled in terms of quality. Production in 1953 stood at 151,323 cars, but this rocketed to 380,561 just four-years later, while crossing the magic first million in August 1955. This 'oval', finished in Horizon Blue, originally destined for the Swedish market, remains more or less original, even down to the very popular period accessory stone-guards on the rear wings. Only the wheels have been incorrectly re-painted!*

Left: *This 1960 Beetle was assembled in South Africa, but with the exception of a different style of headlining, there is little to distinguish it from the Wolfsburg product. Tasteful shades, both external and internal, remained a hallmark, while gradual improvements ensured the Beetle stayed ahead of all opposition.*

Above: *What can words do to add to the appeal of a classic Karmann Ghia? Nothing, other than to advise that the KG was always based on the latest Beetle development, progressing from a 30bhp engine to the more powerful 34bhp unit in August 1960, adopting the 1300 engine in August 1965 and the 1493cc, 44bhp power block 12-months later.*

Left: *The Type 34 was based on VW's larger family saloon, the confusingly named VW 1500 and launched at the same time. Just as the Italian Ghia design studio had been responsible for the elegant lines of the original KG, so they were with the car that came to be known as the 'Razor-Edge'. Most believe that the Type 34's appearance was directed at the US market but sadly, the car was never exported there. Altogether more roomy if not much bigger overall than the Type One Karmann, the car started life with a 1500 engine and progressed to a 1600 unit in later years.*

Here we are in the driver's realm: white de-luxe steering wheel, two rear-view mirrors for increased safety, fully adjustable sun visor, pivoting and sliding windows, heater and defrosters – nothing was forgotten that could make driving easier

This is the vehicle to make you feel at home, with plenty of room to move, a panoramic view from every seat – and what is more – a sunroof which can be fixed in any position; upon application, supplied for the Micro Bus at extra cost, it is standard equipment on the Micro Bus "De Luxe".

The top-hinged door in the rear enables the baggage to be stowed from outside in the generous luggage compartment.

Volkswagen Kombi

Design and construction of the Volkswagen range of Transporters were preceded by consultation with experts from numerous companies, and special consideration was given to their particular transport requirements.
The immense versatility of the various Volkswagen models is the direct outcome of this careful study. Many companies prefer an extra bright loading space, others want the windows converted into display windows or have alternate loads of goods and passengers to handle.
All these firms find the Volkswagen Kombi an eminently useful vehicle, satisfying many requirements: for one thing, side and rear windows help to make the interior of the vehicle into a compartment as bright as day.
For another, they are readily turned into attractive display windows, showing their articles to good advantage.
If alternate transport of goods and passengers is required,
it is a matter of a few seconds to remove or replace the two upholstered benches.
Combined use of the vehicle, of course, is also possible,
with one bench so arranged as to leave a generous loading space in the front or rear. The Kombi is noted for its practical and tasteful fittings.
Driver's cab and body have softly upholstered seats with leatherette covering, that makes for long wear, and are easy to clean.

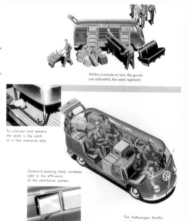

Within a minute or two, the goods are unloaded, the seats replaced.

To unscrew and remove the seats is the work of a few moments only.

Outward-opening body windows add to the efficiency of the ventilation system.

The Volkswagen Kombi, also for simultaneous use with passengers and goods.

Above: *Although the illustration showing an extended family about to depart from what is clearly the grandest of hotels, as evidenced by the uniformed luggage boy loading cases into the boot, is obviously the handiwork of Bernd Reuters, the main illustration might just conceivably emanate from a carefully 'touched-in' photograph, a device VW used to increasing effect as the years went by.*

Left: *The Kombi, the most versatile vehicle in VW's entire range of Transporters, allowed the copywriters to trundle out a bevy of appealing adjectives such as 'useful', 'satisfying', 'attractive', 'practical' and 'tasteful'. Reuters was charged with the task of showing the Kombi as a people carrier, a load-lugging workhorse and as a carefully arranged combination of the two.*

The Pickup demanded an expensive re-tooling exercise and valuable Drawing Office time from the design team, hence its delayed debut. Various panels were unique to its makeup and items like the fuel tank had to be re-sited thanks to its flatbed. The Double Cab Pickup, although designed to be another workhorse, became particularly popular in the USA, where it doubled as a family vehicle, thanks to the increased seating capacity.

Once again, this variant required expensive re-tooling and relied on a number of panels unique to its design. The additional height afforded by the High Roof Model was used by the German Post Office, glaziers and members of the clothing trade. Yet most options leant themselves to a wide variety of applications, hence the rapid development of a market in specials, something Volkswagen was only too happy to accommodate. From mobile shops and libraries to drinks delivery vehicles, catering vans and much more, the options were virtually endless. And it is in this area that the camper van has its place.

The German firm Westfalia had long been producing caravans and camping trailers, but with the launch of the Transporter saw a whole new vista open before them. In 1951, they launched what was known as the 'Camping Box', a relatively spartan box of tricks that could transform a Kombi used for work during the week, into a camper for leisure time. Soon afterwards they introduced 'fitted interiors', which invariably consisted of little more than cupboards and a fold-down bed. However, the notion caught on and within a short time a whole host of different conversions were available, some closer to official sanction than others. In Britain, Lisburne Garage of Torquay was one of the first to latch on to the idea and utilised an established cabinet-making firm based in Sidmouth, (J P White) to create interiors of the very highest standard. The 'Devon' brand, like Topsy, simply grew and grew.

Continual Improvement

Nowadays the number of vans of all marques with an option that lacks a rear window is undoubtedly on the increase, no doubt thanks to ever-increasing attempts by a growing minority to act like magpies, stealing whatever shiny trinkets are on view. VW's Transporter in Panelvan form prior to 21st April 1951 also lacked a rear window, while until November 1950 it sported a massive VW roundel. Amazingly, a rear bumper only became standard on the more basic models in December 1954. To use a little enthusiast's terminology, until March 1955 a massive 'barn-door' gave access to the engine, spare wheel and, of all things, the fuel tank, precariously balanced as it was above the power unit. However, there was strictly no entry to the loading area of the vehicle. The new look, part of a more comprehensive package of modifications, led to the replacement of the 'door' with a much smaller 'lid', which admittedly restricted access to budding mechanics, but allowed the distinct advantage of a separate, top opening, hinged tailgate: so at last the rear luggage area was within instant reach.

Unlike the Beetle, the Transporter was fitted with hydraulic brakes from day one, but it did share a 'crash-box'. Whereas the Beetle benefited from synchromesh on second, third and fourth gears from October 1952, it was March 1953 before this luxury was afforded even to the top of the range options within the Transporter family. However, by the end of the 1950s, it was the commercial vehicle that led the way every time, as it received a full synchromesh box three months ahead of the Beetle. Meanwhile in the engine department, after an upgrade to 30bhp in December 1953, the van was fitted with a brand new and more efficient unit well before such thoughts were transferred to the Beetle.

Both changes occurred in May 1959, although the engine story was rather more complex than it first appears. Amazingly, after calls from customers for more power, VW's new engine was still rated at 30bhp! Stronger crankcase halves, a revised fuel pump drive, re-designed cylinder heads leading to an increase in compression ratio from 6.1:1 to 6.6:1 and even a reduction in the speed of the cooling fan. This may have ensured even greater longevity and a unit that was easier to work on, but it took a further 13-months to boost the horsepower to 34. Once again the compression ratio was raised, this time to 7.0:1, while a new carburettor was fitted, which resulted not only in increased power, but improved acceleration and generally livelier performance.

Hopping back to 1955, not only was the Transporter's rearward appearance altered, so too was the 'up-front' look (both externally and internally). The front of the roof panel was extended to make space for the rudiments of a much-improved fresh air ventilation system. A vent covered with a fine mesh was cut into the underside of the new 'extension', which allowed fresh air to be circulated into a collection box, attached to the underside of the roof panel. The van's occupants could control the airflow with a metal handle fitted to the left hand side of the box.

While it might seem that an excessive number of words have been allocated to something relatively minor, the new 'peak' not only improved the Transporter's aesthetic appearance, but also created a friendlier and less Germanic looking vehicle. Inside, all models received a re-designed (and for the first time in most instances) full-length dashboard of both a more modern and practical application.

Though it might appear logical to assume that what was essentially a face-lifted van in 1955 would have been the product of the new Hanover factory, this was not the case. Wolfsburg alone produced the 'new' Transporter. At the end of 1954, the plant had produced 202,174 vehicles; well short of what it had originally been designed to cater for. However, Nordhoff, ambitious as ever and acutely aware that he was constantly fighting against a shortfall in the number of VWs produced compared to sales requests, commissioned a new factory dedicated to Transporter production. Built at Stöcken, a suburb of Hanover and only 47-miles from Wolfsburg, it offered good communication options but drew on a separate pool of labour.

More Improvements – 1960s Style

The first vehicles had rolled out of Hanover at a rate of 40 per day in March 1956, but by 1959 this figure had increased to the best part of 250. Crucially, not only was the factory purpose built, even down to a railway connecting the plant to the nearby port, but also Hanover came fully equipped with the very latest in both technology and production methods.

As with the Beetle, the antiquated semaphore indicators gave way to a drop of modern technology in March 1960, at the start of the new decade. This change was a portent of what was to come, namely one of changing times demanding upgrades to keep the Transporter competitive in a market place of ever-increasing offerings.

The launch of VW's larger family saloon, the VW 1500 or Type Three, with its 42bhp engine, inspired Nordhoff to pre-empt criticism that the 1200 Transporter was underpowered when compared with its contemporaries, by offering the larger engine where it was most required. Inevitably, the USA was the first country to receive the new engine, which it did in January 1963.

By March of the same year, the 1493cc unit with a top speed of 65mph was also an option in all other markets, but only in versions of the Transporter where 'people carrying' was the main object. Would-be Panelvan owners and Pickup purchasers had to wait until the following August, while the 'basic' 1200 engine soldiered on until the autumn of 1965.

For the 1964 model year, which of course kicked into action in August 1963, the Transporter's tailgate became larger, with the result that the rear window could be made considerably wider. The Samba might have had to lose its enticing wraparound corner glasses, but for the Transporter world at large there was the prospect of a lighter, airier world. Dingy cloth head-linings would also soon disappear, although a truly logical explanation for the move from 15" to 14" wheels, which became standard from just before Christmas in 1963 has never emerged. For the last year of production 12-volt electrics were introduced as standard, having previously been an extra cost option for a four-year period.

Top Left: *Pick-up production began in August 1952 and quickly proved popular, accounting for around 20% of sales. Versatile in the extreme, this hydraulic tipper truck was one of 130 variations listed by VW in 1961 and bore the code S015!*

Middle Left: *The ambulance, always distinguishable by its lack of a rear window, became an official model from December 1951, having previously been produced by coachbuilders, Meisen.*

Bottom Left: *This pre-1955 Microbus, to which someone has added indicators, was the oddest member of the family. Neither basic like a Kombi, or boasting the attributes of its Deluxe brother, it was ideal for transformation into a camper.*

Sales figures held well for the first generation Transporter right until the time that rumours of an impending new model began to emerge. For the 1966 model year 176,275 Transporters had been built. This dropped to 141, 569 in 1967; even so this only took it back to 1960 levels. The new model was launched in August 1967, and the most immediate feature was the van's front end appearance. Gone was the bulbous and sloping tin work, as was the split-screen windscreen. The replacement had a much flatter front end. above which was mounted a one-piece, panoramic windscreen of curved glass.

The change in the windscreen was a really stiking improvement, and such models are now invariably referred to as the 'Bay'. Yet, whilst this was the main element, the new model was undoubtedly bigger, better and crucially more modern in every respect.

As with the 'New Beetle' launched at the same time, Nordhoff was still at the helm, confounding those who have since alleged that Mr Volkswagen was stuck rigidly in the past. However, despite the new model's launch during 1967 and thus before the cut-off point for this study, eager readers will have to await the second instalment of Nostalgia Road's Volkswagen story to appreciate its merits!

A hardworking Devon motor caravan earns its holidays in the sun

Top Right: *Although Volkswagen had not anticipated that their workhorse would become a source of weekend and holiday enjoyment to countless thousands and indeed never became more than tacitly involved in the camping game, an enormous business sprang up in converting both the Kombi and Microbus into camper-vans. Volkswagen endorsed the Westfalia Company in West Germany, whilst here in Britain one of the most popular options was the Devon range, supplied by JP White of Sidmouth, whose literature indicated that their work was 'fully approved by Volkswagenwerk'. At the time the brochure depicted was printed, prices ranged from £950 for the simplest Devon 'Torvette', which was based on the Kombi, to £1,289 for a Devon 'Caravette' using a Deluxe Microbus as the basis for the conversion. Other converters included Canterbury Industrial Products who, despite their name were based in Essex rather than Kent, and who in 1967 were charging between £939 for a Kombi and £1,248 for a Microbus Deluxe minus an elevating roof, for which there was an additional cost of £110. A long list of extras followed, from a cab roof rack to be used in conjunction with the elevating roof at £10, to a 'drive on or off awning tent' at £37 and a spare wash bowl at 4s 11d. Probably most notable of the also-rans was Danbury, again based in Chelmsford. Splitties in general command very high prices today, none more so than the camper conversions.*

Bottom Right: *Who but VW would produce a brochure depicting nothing other than the Transporter in use as a 'Fire Truck'! This photograph, taken in Switzerland, depicts members and a vehicle of the Schinznach-Bad brigade.*

THE SHEEP IN WOLFSBURG CLOTHING!

Even the most casual observer of Volkswagen's air-cooled family must be aware that the convertible, or Cabriolet as it is known in most circles, was rightly the *crème de la crème* of the Beetle range for just about all the long years of German production. From the earliest of days, Porsche had intended that a soft-top version of the KdF-Wagen should be an integral part of the Nazi offering, while the Brits played about with one or two interesting experiments, including the delightfully named Radclyffe 'roadster'.

However, with the arrival of Heinz Nordhoff on the VW scene other priorities, such as turning the Beetle saloon into a saleable product, had to take precedence. A Cabriolet could wait but fortunately, there were at least two coach-building firms in Germany willing to take the strain of producing a luxury soft-top Beetle.

Above: *Volkswagen AG re-released this photograph of the Karmann Ghia as launched in 1955, to coincide with the production of Beetle number 20,000,000 in 1981. The press department's witty caption ran as follows. "The Soft Wave. Messrs Karmann in Osnabrück ... put the Karmann Ghia Coupé on the market. Its flowing shape won it many fans; the Karmann Ghia Coupé became a second car, the cocktail dress of the smart lady."*

One such was Josef Hebmüller and Sons, based at Wülfrath in the Ruhr, who for an all-too brief period were responsible for a delightful two-plus-two Cabriolet before first a fire and then bankruptcy struck. The other keenly interested party was the Osnabrück firm of Wilhelm Karmann, whose origins could be traced back to 1874. Before Nordhoff's appointment, Karmann had pestered sufficiently to be given two Beetles to experiment with as soft-top prototypes.

Amazingly one of these Beetles was the 10,000th car to be built after the war. Sadly, any thought of serious production was aborted due to the lack of materials, such as sheet steel and the fabric required for the hood. As the supply situation improved, Karmann made a further approach and, in May 1949, Nordhoff sanctioned a third prototype, which in turn was followed by 25 pre-production models. In August, Nordhoff placed an order for 2,000 Cabriolets, stipulating that as many Volkswagen components as possible should be used. By the end of the year, Karmann had hand-finished 364 examples, while during April 1950 the 1,000th car left the Osnabrück assembly line.

The pattern was set not only for Karmann to produce soft-top Beetles, incorporating any changes determined for the saloon, which eventually meant taking the top of the range Beetle saloon as the basis for their product, but also for the coach-builder to demonstrate a capability to produce another model altogether, albeit based on the Beetle.

The Karmann Ghia

Despite Nordhoff's reluctance to do anything that would divert vital resources from his goal of building Beetle bastions and his concerns that the somewhat fragile nature of the post-war economic recovery did little to lend itself to the building and sale of an expensive 'sports car', Karmann battered the Director General with proposals until he finally relented. His course of action was to allow Karmann to submit plans and even scale models, each of which was turned over to various heads of department for evaluation.

None of these acquired the sought after approval, that is until Wilhelm Karmann the younger turned almost in desperation to the Italian, Luigi Segre, the commercial director of Carrozeria Ghia. Segre obtained a Beetle, not direct from Wolfsburg as none were available, but via the French concession. Plans were drawn up and the Ghia prototype was shown to Karmann at the Paris auto show, held in October 1953.

Herr Karmann was stunned, for not only had he been expecting a cabriolet, rather than the coupé he was presented with, but also by the sheer beauty of the sporty design. On 16th November, after the tiniest of tweaks, the coupé was presented to Nordhoff and his head of sales, who approved of what they saw. Negotiations followed, with the inevitable result that Karmann would take care of production and final assembly, just as they were doing with the Cabriolet Beetle, while the by now mighty Volkswagen machine would handle the engineering and of course the all-important sales and marketing.

The 'Volkswagen in an Italian sports jacket' (as one advert described the Karmann Ghia) was expensive to build, but the costs of modifying the Beetle it was based on were less than excessive. All that was required was to widen the floor pans by 80mm on both sides, shorten the gear stick to accommodate the sportier and lower seating position and to adjust the steering column.

The real expense came due to the fact that the Karmann works had no large metal presses and the more complicated panels such as the nose cone had to be painstakingly built up out of five smaller panels, each welded together. In total the body required almost four-metres of welding on the outer skin, while every seam had to be filled and finished with lead.

The press launch was fixed for 14th July 1955, partly because the Karmann factory was running out of space, and 37 cars were delivered to dealers in August, although the high profile presentation at the IAA International Car Show held in September increased demand greatly. At 7,500DM the coupé was undoubtedly expensive, particularly when even the Cabriolet version of the Beetle could be had for as little as 5,990DM, thanks to a price cut by Nordhoff, who was in euphoric mood due to the imminent arrival of the millionth saloon.

However, undoubtedly more than in part due to its stylish good looks, the Karmann Ghia soon found its niche in the rapidly growing European sports car market. Remarkably, and despite its inevitably pedestrian performance, sales continued to escalate. From the 1,282 examples built in 1955, 11,555 was the figure for the following year, while by 1960 that had shot up to 19,259, despite the fact that a second variation on the Ghia theme had hit the headlines in September 1957.

Karmann had hankered after building an open two-seater since they first approached Nordhoff. However, simply hacking the roof off the coupé wouldn't do, as the less than rigid remains needed reinforcing. The sills, the area around the 'A' pillar, the vicinity of the sides of the rear seat, all came in for the 'girder' treatment, with the inherent performance penalty, amounting to two mph off the top speed. Inevitably, the finished product though was the epitome of sartorial elegance.

Unlike the Beetle Cabriolet, the Ghia's hood when down disappeared behind the seats, although this in turn restricted luggage space. The top itself, crafted like the Beetle Cabriolet's, from a combination of wool-cloth, mohair and insulating horsehair was far beyond the specification of the average production sports car, although unlike the Beetle the rear 'window' was made of Perspex. Above all, the hood was very easy to manoeuvre both up and down.

Production of the Karmann Ghia convertible began in August 1957, while at launch the following month it cost just 750DM more than the coupé, coming in as it did at 8250DM. With the least expensive Porsche at the time costing 12,600DM, it had to be in with a chance of considerable success. On a more negative note the 1958 model year Beetle Cabriolet cost just 5990DM! While production never came near to the lofty heights of its tin-top sister it was nevertheless popular. From the 4,392 cars produced in its first full year, compared to 14,515 coupes, production hovered at a little over the 5,000 mark until the late 1960s, when in excess of 6,000 were built annually. A little over 70% of all cars produced were destined for the lucrative US market.

Improving the Product

There is little to say about the Karmann Ghia's performance or its mechanical development over the years, as most issues have already been covered under the Beetle heading. As such, the Ghia started life with the trusty 30bhp engine, graduated to the 34bhp unit alongside the Beetle for the 1961 model year, experienced a brief dalliance with the 1285cc, 40bhp unit and by the time Heinz Nordhoff died it was sporting the 1493cc top of the range power unit.

Disc brakes arrived at the same time as the 44bhp motor, nearly 11-years after the Karmann Ghia first saw the light of day. All this conservative Beetle technology led one sports car magazine of the day to openly (cynically) write that the only reason the Volkswagen Karmann Ghia was included between its covers was due to its shape!

Above: *Volkswagen's 20-million pack contained this shot of the Karmann Ghia Convertible. The caption sums up the mood: - "Karmann Ghia's success with the coupé led to the next logical step, the two-seater Karmann Ghia convertible an exclusive alternative for sun-worshipping wind-in-the-hair drivers."*

Having admitted that the KG's performance was unquestionably pedestrian compared to its appearance, nevertheless it at least gave the illusion to owners of being more agile than its bug-like cousin. Likewise, the body with its interior width of 1400mm compared to the Beetle's at 1250mm, felt both comfortable and roomy, although items such as the steering wheel, the ashtray and even the speedometer, were taken straight form the Beetle's parts bin. However, from day one it featured indicators rather than semaphores, while the dash was adorned with the odd supplementary items, like a large and highly prominent clock.

The seats were particularly well upholstered and offered initially in cloth, although both leatherette and a radio were extra cost options. In 1959, for the 1960 model year, the Karmann Ghia received its first face-lift. The headlamps were positioned 45mm higher and further forward on re-designed wings, leading enthusiasts to describe the earlier models as 'low light Ghias'. The bumpers were also re-positioned but, most strikingly, the elegant 'nostrils' adjacent to the front 'cone' were re-shaped and made both longer and larger.

At the rear of the car, the light clusters were enlarged, while wider door glasses, larger wheel arches and hinged side windows, all helped to distinguish the new from the old, no doubt of great significance to those who wished to keep up with the proverbial Jones's! Improved sound insulation and a dashboard with the upper part padded were undoubtedly worthwhile enhancements.

In 1966, Karmann added two-speed wipers to the package, but this was only a copy of Beetle upgrades. Redesigned front seats and a modified interior were perhaps more important, but essentially the elegance of the original body shape was still responsible for an encouraging sales level of 24,729 coupés and 5,713 convertibles in the year of Nordhoff's death.

Top Right: *Although the main thrust of the chapter of the book might be about the Karmann Ghia, who would miss the opportunity to reproduce some of Reuters's brilliant artwork to promote the first product Karmann were associated with. This mid-1950s Cabriolet brochure's cover conveys the open-air freedom a soft top provides through the single image of the driver's windswept hair. VW were careful to describe the Cabriolet in both words and pictures as an option most suited to the ladies.*

Middle Right: *This photograph appeared in a brochure printed in 1963 and nearly a decade after the KG's launch. Compared with the car as launched in 1955, the most notable difference is at the front end. The headlamps now sat higher by some two-inches on the wings, while the 'nostrils', allowing fresh air to enter the KG's interior, were enlarged. The change occurred in August 1959, for the 1960 model year, and was initiated to meet international standards.*

Bottom Right: *Photographed in 1983, at what has since become one of the premier VW events held each year, this Karmann Coupe could easily be mistaken for the one depicted in the brochure picture that we have presented above. More or less hand-finished, the price of the Karmann Ghia was always relatively expensive when compared to the Beetle on which it was based. Primarily it was a two-seater although there was cramped accommodation in the rear for children. The interior width however was 185mm better than that of the Beetle, but luggage space was severely restricted.*

THIRD TIME LUCKY?

The big problem with the new car Volkswagen launched officially in September 1961 was its name. Officially described as the VW 1500, it was an identity that became very confusing by the time Volkswagen launched the 1493cc version of the Beetle as the VW 1500! At this point, six years into production, the top of the range models had been designated as VW 1600s for just 12-months, while the base cars had retained the VW 1500 designation to the exact point the Beetle took on its mantle!

As a result, most enthusiasts and anyone else who can recall the Beetle's bigger brother, refer to the car as the Type Three. This adopts the factory's own method of designation, following in the footsteps of the Beetle and its derivatives, (Type One) and the Transporter (Type Two).

A fallacy has been perpetuated for many years that the Type Three was conceived as a replacement for the Beetle, whose design in 1957, when the notion of a Type Three was first considered, was already over 20-years old. However, apart from the obvious fact that Nordhoff couldn't produce enough Beetles to match demand and therefore was hardly likely to turn his attention to a replacement, the Type Three, although it shared its brother's floor-pan, was altogether a bigger affair, ideal for family motoring. Nordhoff was aware that those wishing to graduate from the confines of the people's car had nothing to turn to other than the products of rival manufacturers.

Speaking in Switzerland in March 1960, Nordhoff predicted that by the end of the year he would be producing "4,000 Volkswagens daily." He added, "then we believe we shall have reached a balance between supply and demand, so that we can finally deliver Volkswagens to customers without a waiting period."

He might have gone on to say that at such a point the time would be right to address the question of a larger family saloon, save that such a project was still supposedly a secret. However, he did hint at just such a model before a prolonged game of hide and seek began with motoring journalists.

The other misconception still frequently repeated is that the Type Three was a failure. Admittedly, when compared to sales of the Beetle, the levels were paltry, but what rival manufacturer's offering wasn't. It also has to be taken into account when tallying up the totals, that the Type Three wasn't available in the United States (potentially one of its biggest markets) until 1965.

When production finally ended in 1973, more than 2,500,000 Type Threes had been sold, far more than many a car deemed to be a success both in its time and today.

Below: *By the beginning of 1963, when this brochure was produced, VW felt confident enough to issue photographs of their 'new' product depicting less than the whole vehicle. Read the text though and the reasoning is clear – the message was one of room and space.*

It's a new Volkswagen, the VW 1500 Sedan. A car that has more room than our VW. And more power. And more comfort. But it's still a Volkswagen. With all of Volkswagen's famous engineering features and a few more besides.
The new, rugged 1.5 I engine (with 53 hp) is rear mounted and air cooled (of course). The

gearbox is fully synchronized (mais oui). The wheels are individually suspended by torsion bars (naturlich).
The VW 1500 accommodates up to five people (and their luggage) very comfortably.
In fact, ther are two luggage compartments, one in the front under the bonnet, the other in back. (13.4 cubic feet altogether.)

Both are accessible from outside.
Where's the engine?
It's hidden under the rear luggage compartment. Its unique flat construction makes an additional luggage compartment possible.

It's a VW 1500 Convertible. A car you can get a lot into. Here you see the two luggage compartments- front and rear.
Like all other Volkswagen convertibles, the side windows wind down completely and the padded, double top opens and closes with ease. Something extra special in convertibles-the rear window is made of safety glass. Like all VW

1500s, the car offers even more: a paddeed, non-reflecting dashboard, instruments (petrol guage and clock) with padded cowl. Push buttons for headlight, windscreen wiper and windscreen washer, roomy door pockets, comfortable arm rests on both doors.
Thats only the beginning. The car has three ashtrays, two padded sun vizors that pivot

sideways, and a passneger grab handle.
The floor is covered with rubber matting, the sides are finished with vinyl. Everything is fully washable.
Its all standard equipment-no extra charge.

The VW 1500, Type Three At Launch

Conservatively modern in its styling, the Type Three more or less shared its floor-pan with that of the Beetle. However, the body at 4225mm was some 160mm longer than that of the Type One. It also benefited from two larger luggage areas and offered its occupants more elbow room as, unlike the Beetle, it didn't get any narrower towards the front.

The interior shared the simplicity of its smaller brother, although it did offer three round gauges, the centre one being a speedometer, while to the left there was one to record fuel, which also was home to various indicator lights for anything as diverse as full beam to oil pressure. To the right was a clock. The upper part of the dashboard was appropriately padded.

Unlike some of its potential rivals, the Type Three was only ever available as a two-door vehicle, although pop-out rear side windows were standard. Inevitably visibility was good and thanks to various measures, like rubber dampers between the body and what amounted to a sub-frame, the Type Three suffered little road noise or vibration. Worm and roller steering with steering dampers ensured decent road holding and handling.

The car's three-box section appearance, a possibility thanks only to a re-working of the flat four engine, more of which shortly, earned it the name of 'notchback', terminology by which the saloon is still referred to today.

Above: *Although a convertible version of the VW 1500 was shown at the launch, it never went into production, due to insurmountable structural problems. However, as late as the beginning of 1963, the brochure men were still including it with the rest of the range. Inevitably, a collector will now snap up any material showing the VW 1500 convertible!*

The Type Three boasted two boots, one up-front carrying 180dm^3 and another at the back offering a further 200dm^3. Re-arranging the engine components created this extra space, so that a horizontal draught carburettor was employed, while the fan was attached to the crankshaft instead of the crankcase. The overall height of the engine came to just 38cm, and as it was positioned low down at the rear of the chassis the effect was noticeable. The engine's output was restricted so that it would last a long time, but it still offered 45bhp at 3800rpm. Well-spaced gearing gave great potential for overtaking, acceleration times and the top speed of 82mph were both significantly better than that of the Beetle.

With effect from February 1962 two variant models of the Type Three were added to the notchback offering, one could carry 375kg and the other 460kg, thanks to an additional torsion bar. This was VW's attempt to wrestle a little away from Opel's near stranglehold on the station wagon, or estate car market. Identical as far as the 'B' pillar, the variant was more adaptable than the saloon and its appearance possibly more attractive.

Top Left: *For some time it had been widely known that Volkswagen was planning to add an extra model to its line-up of the Beetle, Transporter and Karmann Ghia. As a matter of fact Heinz Nordhoff himself had hinted as much at the 1960 Geneva Car Show. His original intention of making VW the largest automobile company in Europe had been accomplished and at last Volkswagen could match Beetle production to sales. Now Nordhoff not only needed to challenge the recent impact made by US-owned car-makers (Ford and General Motors) on the German market, but to demonstrate that VW was much more than a one brand company. The VW 1500, or Type Three was his answer and at the launch in 1961 there were various options available, a complete range almost from day one. While the new car was not a Beetle, it shared the principles that made it a Volkswagen. Sales of the VW 1500 in its first full year totalled 127,324, in 1963 that had grown to 181,809 and in 1964 to 262,020. Before the recession of 1967, Nordhoff could be content with a figure of 311,701 VW 1600s sold.*

Bottom Left: *The VW 1500S, introduced in August 1963, featured more chrome and more power thanks to its twin-carburettors, but sold at exactly the same price as its predecessor. The new car ofered a 0-60mph time of 18.8 seconds from its 54bhp engine. However, some markets resisted its notchback appearance, preferring the variant as both more attractive and practical, while later they would line up in rows to select the fastback depicted opposite.*

One of the VW air-cooled world's biggest enigmas was closely connected with the Type Three, for at the notchbacks' first airing at Frankfurt in September 1961, it shared the platform with a convertible version, carefully created by Karmann.

To modern eyes at least, the soft top was exceptionally bland, because Karmann had taken care to use standard panels everywhere below the waistline in order to keep prices down. Although the hood did fold away completely without compromising the space available to rear seat passengers, perhaps it was not what was expected of a firm responsible for the Karmann Ghia and even the Beetle Cabriolet.

Nevertheless, Volkswagen pushed ahead with the convertible, announcing a price of 8,200DM and printing the necessary brochures to promote it. As late as January 1963 the convertible was still appearing in print with a brochure entitled, "What kind of car is a Volkswagen?"

A brief extract suffices to tell the story: "like all other Volkswagen convertibles, the side windows wind down completely and the padded double top opens with ease. Something extra special in convertibles – the rear window is made of glass …".

However, a major problem relating to the body's torsional rigidity could not be solved and inevitably the project was finally (and quietly) dropped.

Improving The Product 1960s Style

The 1964 model year saw the Type Three as it had been produced before reduced in status to 'N' level and the introduction of 'S' models in both notchback and variant form. Such vehicles were endowed with a second carburettor, increasing the maximum output to 54bhp at 4200rpm, while 0-60 acceleration times dropped to 18.8 seconds. Externally the 'S' models were laden with additional chrome, but the big news was that the price was exactly that of the previous model at 6,400DM, which in turn fell to just 5,990DM.

In August 1965, for the 1966 model year the 1500S was replaced with the 1600TL, while the 'N' designation was changed to an 'A'. A year later, out went the 1500A to be replaced by the 1600A. Complicated, not a bit of it! The 'TL' designation stood for 'tourenlimousine'.

Above: *With the 1966 model year came more changes to the Type Three range, the most significant of which was the appearance of a fastback. However, the other news, was yet another engine upgrade, undoubtedly aimed at warding off far more powerful competition than the Beetle had to face.*

The new car completely transformed the Type Three's appearance, for now the rear sloped away, almost as a precursor of the 1970s hatchback icon. Known as the 'fastback' the conservative looks of the original Type Three were swept away with this new sporty looking model. Coupled to this improvement was the arrival of a brand new engine, the 1600, or 1584cc 54bhp engine that would push the Volkswagen forward better at the lower speeds demanded in increasingly busy towns, while crucially using regular rather than premium fuel. For the 1967 model year, all models benefited from the introduction of 12-volt electrics.

The Type 34

If ever there was an author's dilemma, this is it. Should VW's Type 34 be added to the Karmann chapter as a true product of the Osnabrück factory, but as a child of the 1960s and thus destroy the continuity of the overall story? Does a car that merited just 42, 498 sales warrant a chapter of its own? Or should the Type 34, whose very designation links it inextricably to the Type Three, be tagged on to the appropriate chapter? The answer is clear for the Type 34 was the fourth variation of the new VW 1500, after the notchback, the enigmatic convertible and, of course, the variant.

While Karmann's team were busy hacking the top off the Type Three, the design brief for the additional model was handed once more to Ghia, this time to the creative skills of one Sergio Sartorelli. Apparently angled towards the American taste; gone was the classic and elegant styling of the original Karmann Ghia, to be replaced by an aggressive creation full of sharp edges and modern statements. Having said that the Karmann Ghia was at least balanced, with its long front end matching an equally lengthy rear. Its large, though near vertical windscreen, plus the sharply sloping rear pane, gave it a feeling of luxury, if elegance wasn't the first word that came to mind regarding its overall appearance.

The unusual 'hooded' stance of the front end, coupled with the very American look of the circular rear lamp lenses made the car quirky to say the very least. Although it appeared enormous by comparison with the Beetle based Karmann Ghia, in reality although it was indeed some 140mm longer, it was slightly less wide, while it also sat closer to the ground but defied logic with an overall height 10mm greater than its popular cousin. Today, at least in enthusiast circles, the Type Three Karmann Ghia is invariably referred to as the 'Razor Edge', a highly appropriate nickname for this most unusual of Volkswagens.

Initially reactions to the car were excellent and in November 1961 mass production began, although a proposed Cabriolet version with a retail price tag of 9,500DM against the coupé's 8,750DM ticket, never saw the light of day. In engine terms the Type Three KG always ran with the top of the range option. At launch, thanks to its 'sleek' lines, the top speed was seven-kph more than that of the notchback. During its lifetime, apart from engine upgrades, the Ghia acquired, amongst other items, a dashboard covered in a wood grain film (that few seemed to like) and better stopping power, which was met with near universal approval, when front discs became the norm. However, once Nordhoff had been replaced at Castle Wolfsburg the Type Three Karmann Ghia's future seemed less than secure and in July 1969 it was the first of the air-cooled models to be chopped unceremoniously out of the range.

Top, Middle & Bottom Left: *Three images of the Type 34: a fully restored 1965 costing its owner £1,391 2s 11d, a daily driver from the 1970s and a cutaway revealing luggage carrying capabilities!*

END GAME

Three new air-cooled models appeared after the death of Heinz Nordhoff, all of which the great man had undoubtedly had a hand in, but of which only one could really be described as his legacy.

Of least significance was the Type 181, launched in August 1969. During the 1960s the West German army had an ever-increasing need to replace, or at least supplement their long-in-the-tooth four-wheel drive vehicle. Volkswagen were contracted to design and develop the new offering. The result, a wartime Kübel-like replica, based on the Karmann Ghia floor pan, but otherwise almost pure Beetle, may or may not have been considered appropriate by Nordhoff as a commercially viable vehicle, we shall never know.

As the first prototype of the VW-Porsche 914 was only ready 15-days before Nordhoff collapsed and later died, its final form and the marketing strategy exercised had little if anything to do with him. However, in the autumn of 1966 when Nordhoff was still very much in control, he had met with Ferry Porsche, to discuss the possibility of a joint project between the two companies to build an affordable, open two-seater, aimed primary at the American market.

Devoid of the Type 34 there, VW were conscious they were missing out to others, such as MG, who sold 12,000 MGBs that year. Porsche were to be the designers, while in order to keep the costs down as many VW parts would be used as possible.

The VW 411, a family saloon launched in October 1968, was the largest air-cooled Volkswagen, measuring 4.6metres and was revolutionary in terms of Wolfsburg design thoughts at least. Lacking a separate chassis, it boasted MacPherson struts and coil springs, instead of VW's normal reliance on torsion bars. Pininfarina had been offered an advisory contract with Volkswagen and is credited with the basic look of the vehicle, albeit that VW's own team clearly tweaked it a little to placate the conservative nature of their customer database.

The engine was a new 1679cc, 68bhp unit featuring alloy pistons in a cast iron block. Dual carburettors, something Nordhoff had resisted for the Beetle, but not later Type Three models, gave it that 'go-faster' feeling. The boot was at the front, but there was also a recess available behind the rear seats, creating a weight distribution package as near perfect as possible. The 411 was the first Volkswagen to boast four doors, at least in saloon form and was launched both as a base model and with deluxe trim, not to mention an automatic; in other words almost like an offering from Opel or any of the other rivals to Volkswagen's crown. Crucially at launch, it was described as 'pure Nordhoff' despite its much more modern characteristics.

Below: *From a brochure launching the new 411, enthusiasm abounds! "The fastest, most exciting ... most comfortable car ever to come from Volkswagen ... luxury car luxury ... the chassis of a sports car and a unitized all-steel body, for safety's sake. ... a powerful 76bhp engine..."*

Set to meet the next decade?

Nordhoff left his successor at Volkswagen with a healthy, profitable company. In 1968 any notion of the decline in VW's fortunes in the USA, its most important export market, could be scotched as the Beetle recorded its best year ever with sales of 390,079 cars. While the Beetle had been substantially revised and 1,186,134 would be built that year, the Transporter boasted a whole new incarnation. Production was up by some 33% over the last complete year of Splittie sales.

The Type Three had not long been upgraded, both with a more powerful engine and through the introduction of the fastback. A production level of 244,427 cars was not to be sniffed at. Even the niche market Karmann Ghia suddenly took a leap forward after years of steady sales. Additionally, there was the imminent prospect of an even larger family saloon and variant. Crucially, profit stood at 339 million DM, or 543 million with the satellites taken into consideration.

Sadly, the new man at the top, Kurt Lotz had very different ideas regarding Volkswagen's future, both immediate and long-term. The next part of the Volkswagen story traces the fate of the air-cooled models and attempts to demonstrate why it might have been oh so different, had Nordhoff survived and worked for another decade.

Below: *The VW passenger car line up for the final year covered here and the end of the Nordhoff era, a truly Golden Age in Volkswagen's history. From the humble 1200 Beetle – the 'Sparkafer', through the various Type Three options, to the implied opulence of the products produced by Karmann. This should have been a recipe for continued success. From a workforce of 8,719 when Nordhoff arrived in 1948 and a total of 19,244 cars produced, in the year of his death the German factories alone employed 104,975 people and produced 1,548,933 vehicles. Over 30-years later, the workforce is similar but, despite rapid advances in technology, makes fewer cars, with a figure of 956,617 being produced in 2002.*

Our principle has always been to steadily improve each and every Volkswagen. To make them safer and safer. More and more comfortable. Better and better value for money. Which is just what we've done this year, too.
Here's the new VW programme:

VW 1200 – the best VW ever for the money.
VW 1300 – comfortably equipped with many extras at no extra charge.

VW 1500 – as comfortable as the VW 1300 but with a more powerful engine and disc brakes up front.
VW Automatic – the Beetle you drive better and more safely in – automatically.
VW 1600 A – the most favourably priced VW in the 1.6 litre class.
VW Variant 1600 A – the large, economical family car. With room and to spare for both passengers and luggage.

VW 1600 L – the elegant saloon with the elegant interior and a wealth of fitting and fixtures.
VW 1600 TL – the fastback saloon with sports car performance. And generously proportioned interior.
VW Variant 1600 L – the large, elegant and spacious family saloon.
VW 1500 Convertible – the four-seater convertible which is always fun to drive. Even in winter.
VW 1500 Karmann Ghia Coupé – as lively and elegant as a sports car. And much roomier.

VW 1500 Karmann Ghia Convertible – just as lively and elegant. Just as weatherproof thanks to its heavily padded, waterproof top.
VW 1600 L Karmann Ghia Coupé – the large, fast VW Coupé with the thoroughbred lines. Luxurious. Spacious.
All these Volkswagens are individually equipped and differently priced. Each has its own special cachet. But more important still is what they all have in common: VW Quality, VW Economy and VW Service.

VOLKSWAGEN MOTORS LIMITED.

To conclude the Volkswagen story in the years up to April 1968 and the death of Heinz Nordhoff, some attempt needs to be made to look at the phenomenally successful export drive, without which the Beetle and therefore VW, wouldn't have become the success it undoubtedly did. While one of the most fascinating tales imaginable and desperate struggles possible to gain an initial foothold in the unquestionably lucrative US market might appear to be the logical example; the *Classic Marques* series quite naturally is geared towards cars offered in Britain. As such, what better alternative could there be than to assess the tangled hotchpotch that amounted to the birth of VW in this country.

The Volkswagen story in Britain kicked in comparatively late, possibly due to the invader's reluctance to tackle the country whose automobile industry had pioneered work in small car production with obvious success.

Above: *Probably the most famous Beetle in Britain, known by its registration plate to enthusiasts far and wide, JLT 420 was built in 1947, a product of the British period of control at Wolfsburg. Curious then, it was such a car, almost a 'grey import' that may have been responsible for the term 'Beetle'. Rumour has it that when garage owner, John Colborne Baber used the car for a short period after acquiring it, taking his son to and collecting him from school, other pupils would call out, 'Here comes Baber in his Beetle', no doubt thanks to the car's 'bug-like' shape.*

Strangely, whilst more small cars were produced in Britain than anywhere else in the world, Nordhoff realised that the British public were partially starved of cars, due to the home industry's export drive, which then accounted for 70% of total production. Despite this chink in the Bulldog's armour another factor simmered in the background, which many years later helps to clarify why Britain wasn't at the top of Volkswagen's shopping list.

Top Left: *The firm of AA Mauleverer Ltd, of Bournemouth sold the Metallic Blue Deluxe car seen here and on the cover of this book. Built on 15th October 1953, it was nearly a month later before the car was shipped from Wolfsburg to Britain, raising speculation that sales in the first months were less than Nordhoff had anticipated. This car was first registered on 1st December 1953, and eight-days later it passed into the hands of its first owner, who kept the Beetle for the best part of 20-years. After a brief period with a lady owner, the next name recorded on the logbook used the car until his death. The Beetle was advertised in the VW press in the spring of 1981, allowing enthusiasts to gain access to its whereabouts. It was snapped up and brought over 200-miles north, where it remained in the same hands until the beginning of this century. Little has been needed in the way of restoration work and it still runs on its original 25bhp motor.*

Bottom Left: *'The Internationally famous Volkswagen' shouts the headline of the advert placed to promote the Beetle's presence at Earls Court Motor Show in the autumn of 1953. Sadly the early days of the British operation might best be described as bordering on a shambles, resulting in under 1,000 cars being sold in the first year and with losses incurred as a result.*

Pronounced anti-German feelings remained reasonably strong even as late as the mid-1950s. The vandalism to shipments of newly imported Beetles waiting at Harwich docks, at one point rose to an incredible rate of three out of every four cars lined up! However, such sentiments were appreciated and handled with Nordhoff's customary caution.

Before 1953, which is the year when Volkswagen Motors Limited set up an office at Inego Place, Bedford Street, London, there had been some activity, albeit of a less than official nature. John Colborne-Baber was operating from premises in Ripley, Surrey when a Swedish gentleman turned up on his forecourt with a Volkswagen, the first such car Colborne-Baber had seen. The Swede wanted to buy a Buick that was on offer, but problems arose, as nobody knew the true value of the German product.

Eventually a sum of £150 was agreed upon. Colborne-Baber decided to use the vehicle himself for a short time and was suitably impressed, declaring that here 'was a small saloon you could drive like a sports car' and that 'this vehicle was streets ahead of anything [he] had ever driven in the small car class'. The decision was taken to specialise in the Volkswagen and adverts were placed in motoring journals offering to buy the spare parts packs supplied to anybody taking a Beetle out of Germany. The cars themselves tended to be obtainable from the same people who held the packs, Control Commission personal who had returned to Britain.

As the Beetles of the day were far from perfect in terms of finish, Colborne-Baber gutted them, re-upholstered the seats in leather, which by a fluke of the tax rules was cheaper than Rexene and then resprayed the body to the customer's choice of colour.

Good fortune means that the invoice for the work carried out on the very first Beetle has survived and makes interesting reading, albeit that the standard pattern for refurbishment hadn't evolved.

"To beating out all dents in wings and bonnet, repairing tear in rear squab and attending to interior trimming where necessary. Fitting polished aluminium on floor edges. Removing horn, straightening and chromium plating bumpers. Stopping, filling and completely recellulosing (sic) red … £65."

Top Right: *Enclosed with each brochure handed out, the 1953 price list showed that the Beetle wasn't a cheap option.*

Middle Right: *The original owner of the 1956 model year Jungle Green Sunroof Deluxe, pondered for some time before finally deciding to purchase the car that would provide her transport for the next 40-years. Amongst the items handed over to the second owner was a brochure covering the relevant model year and a copy of a magazine article reviewing the 'new' Beetle. VW Motors of Byrom House, 7-9 James Street, London SW1, presented an invoice totalling £788 17s 0d, a sum which included an iniquitous purchase tax levy of £263 17s 0d. A separate invoice was presented for number plates, the amount payable being a princely £1 10s 0d. The only other item to have survived those earliest of days was a charming dealer prepared key-fob. When the car was eventually sold, it had only covered 32,000 miles. With the exception of the normal parking knocks to the wings and subsequent tidying and respray work, the bodywork remains coated with the same paint as that applied at Wolfsburg in 1955.*

Bottom Right: *Built on 8th April 1960, this Jupiter Grey Standard model arrived in Britain just five days later. VW distributor, Moortown Motors of Leeds sold it to a customer in Guiseley and it was registered on 6th May. The garage fixed a small metal plaque to the passenger door, not far from the quarter-light to proclaim its heritage. For the next 26-years and 68,000 miles, the car remained with the original owner. It is alleged that he never washed the VW, preferring to clean off any dirt with a cloth! Following his death at the age of 81, it soon passed into the hands of the author. Frequent references have been made throughout to the Deluxe or Export Beetle, far fewer to the Standard. When this car was built, total annual production of the base model accounted for less than 3% of all sales, while in Britain such cars were if anything even rarer! Even as late as 1960, the Standard still came with cable brakes, while changing gear was accomplished without synchromesh. Externally such cars lacked most of the trim associated with the Deluxe, including bonnet badges and VW roundels. Although 'British' Standard models benefited from chromed bumpers and hubcaps, the home market and some export destinations suffered simple painted items.*

VOLKSWAGEN LIST PRICE

	BASIC PRICE	PURCHASE TAX	TOTAL PRICE
STANDARD SALOON	£458 0 0	£191 19 2	£649 19 2
DE LUXE SALOON	£521 0 0	£218 4 2	£739 4 2
DE LUXE SUNROOF SALOON	£545 0 0	£228 4 2	£773 4 2

(ALL PRICES EX LONDON)

 VW MOTORS LTD.

Head Office :
BYRON HOUSE,
7-9 St. JAMES'S STREET,
LONDON, S.W.I.
Telephone : WHitehall 5901 - 10 lines

Spare Parts Dept.:
79-85 DAVIES STREET,
LONDON, W.I.
Telephone : MAYfair 6718

Above: *Built on 10th October 1961 and despatched from Wolfsburg just five days later, this Turquoise Deluxe is most remarkable for the number of period accessories it now sports. The first owner was a resident of Stanway, a suburb of Colchester in Essex. This explains the seemingly unusual '00' plate, which was at the beck and call of the County authority. First registered on 25th January 1962, the car didn't change hands until 22nd February 1983 following the death of the original keeper. The car had several drivers after this before it fell into the hands of the current owner, who set about a light restoration in 1989, following the attention of vandals. Curiously, this owner was approached by someone who had recognised the car from the time when he had worked at Merit Motors. This firm was the original dealer, who had given the car its PDI (Post Delivery Inspection) prior to its first registration. Accessories fitted include gearshift and ignition locks, windscreen deflectors, rear window Venetian-style visor, headlamp 'eyebrows', jack-plugs, and a spare wheel tool kit.*

The first 'British' car, known far and wide by its registration plate, JLT 420, re-appeared on the Colborne-Baber forecourt some 20-years later, where, with an additional 200,000 miles on the clock, it was snapped up for £100 and after due restoration has remained a showpiece for the garage ever since. By 1951, Colborne-Baber's refurbished Beetles were selling for £410 and, if converted to right-hand-drive, for an extra £15, or £425.

During the course of the following year, 1952, he had been granted a limited and restricted licence to import cars and parts for Americans based in the country. Altogether, probably 20 new cars were sold prior to 1953, while 100-plus refurbished examples passed through the garage's hands in the years between 1948 and 1952. Heinz Nordhoff reasoned that the best way to ensure successful penetration of the British market would be to create a British concession, run entirely by British management, who could introduce the Beetle in their own familiar and inimitable style. Two possible candidates emerged to take responsibility for such an operation and both already had associations with Volkswagen.

Inevitably, Colborne-Baber was one, but the other (Dubliner Stephen O'Flaherty) had the stronger credentials. Joining the motor trade in the 1930s, O'Flaherty had worked for Ford in Cork. After the war he decided to go into business for himself gradually adding a whole cavalcade of brands to his list of imports. His first meeting with Nordhoff took place shortly after the latter had taken over at Wolfsburg and by 1950 he had formed Volkswagen Distributors Limited of Long Mile Road, Dublin. The Irish Republic was to be the first place in the world where CKD kits were assembled. Although O'Flaherty scooped the big prize, Colborne-Baber received some sort of compensation in the form of an eight-county distributorship, at least for the time being.

Realising the scale of investment, O'Flaherty recognised a partnership had to be established and he joined with K J Dear and Stanley Grundy; the former acting as Managing Director to O'Flaherty's role as corporate Chairman. A temporary office but no showroom was finally established in June, six months after the concession had been granted on 1st January 1953. One month and one move later, with press notices having confirmed the formation of Volkswagen Motors Ltd, a string of would-be dealers and distributors began arriving at what was little more than an eight by six foot office above the Lotus showrooms in Regent Street.

Top Right: *This Deluxe Beetle was built on 11th November 1961, but it wasn't registered until 22nd March 1963. The dealership handling the sale was the Walter Scott Motor Company, who had premises in both North and Central London. A director of the company, who also happened to be a relation of the purchaser, handed the keys of the new car over to its first lady owner. She was to use it for the next 26 years until a combination of failing health and old age persuaded her to stop driving; the car had covered just 17,000 miles in all those years!*

Middle Right: *First registered on 13th December 1966, Black and White Garages of Harvington, Worcestershire sold this 1500 to a local gentleman who drove it until his death in 1977. His widow kept it for a further 13 years, during which time the number of miles recorded on the speedometer grew to a little over 70,000. In March 1990 the car became the property of an enthusiast who carried out a thorough Concours winning restoration, although to many it already looked near perfect.*

Top Right: *VW dealers, S L Green of Faldingworth, Lincolnshire must have been delighted to have one regular customer on their books at least. Every three years, when the prospect of an MOT arose, the original owner of this 1967 base model, finished in Fontana Grey (L595), rushed to Green's and bought another new car. Following the private sale of this car to an enthusiast, it changed hands once more when the prospect of a special addition arose. Since 1972, the car has been with its current owner and has now covered well over the 100,000 miles figure.*

Above: *While it might appear a little strange to include a Transporter in a classic line-up, it does serve to remind readers that not all VW fans, or would be buyers, chose the ubiquitous Beetle. Built on 27th April 1964 at the Hanover factory, before it was offered for sale in this country the Transporter was converted by the firm of Canterbury to camper status, with a package that included both an elevating roof that was home to two-bunks, and a built in sink unit. A gentleman from Hayes in Middlesex traded in his eight-year old, 1956 model, Morris Oxford, earning himself an allowance of £175 against the full purchase price of the new van, which stood at £1043 8s 10d. Griffin Motors of Uxbridge were the vendors. Consult an appropriate listing of dealers and distributors for the year and there they are, entered under Hillingdon – Griffin Motors (Uxbridge), Uxbridge Road, Middlesex. Tel Uxbridge 8331! The van remained with its original owner for 18-years, during which time the engine was replaced after a kind gesture to help a fellow camper out of thick mud went wrong, causing terminal damage to the power plant. After five-years with the original owner's son-in-law, the Transporter passed into the hands of an enthusiast.*

That so many were interested in becoming involved with VW is explained by two factors, one of which has already been touched upon. The shortage of the home-built product caused more than a few to simply sign up for an additional option, safe in the knowledge that people would buy come what may, rather than be without reliable personal transport. Secondly, the post-war failure of the Jowett Automobile Company, based in Bradford, Yorkshire had progressively left its dealers without cars to sell, with the inevitable result that many responded to the press notices released about the formation of Volkswagen Motors Limited.

By the early 1960s, about a quarter of the former Jowett dealers were flying the Volkswagen flag on their forecourts. Conversely, and sadly for Volkswagen, many of the top dealers in a given town or city had little option but to disregard the German import and its new British satellite, as they would have lost their existing franchise if they were to sell the Beetle. Inevitably therefore, the construction of the network was somewhat *ad hoc*, with interested parties approaching the new company rather than it exercising a carefully planned strategy, which would have resulted in the evolution of an ideal network. Problems lay ahead as a result!

Top & Bottom Right: *In January 1964 Volkswagen Motors Ltd updated their scale of service and repair charges. The preamble ran as follows: "It is our sincere desire that the excellent performance and economical operation of your Volkswagen will justify the confidence you have placed in our firm when purchasing this new car." Every conceivable operation possible was then listed. Here are a few examples. Remove and install engine - £1 8s 7d: Clutch cable remove and install - £1 10s 10d: Hand brake adjust 6s 7d: Four wheels remove and install, including rotate wheels and correct tyre pressure 5s 6d.*

Middle Right: *Accessories were widely available, as we will discuss later, for example the roof rack shown here was not especially cheap as it would have cost £5 19s 6d. At this time, the national average wage in Britain was £12 11s 3d a week, so a roof rack would account for around half the average man's weekly income and a purchase was not therefore a decision that many families would take lightly.*

During the course of July 1953, Wolfsburg pre-empted any further delays in getting the operation off the ground by demanding to know how many cars were required to fulfil, the fledgling's initial order. With O'Flaherty absent more often than he was present and the chaos of establishing a dealer network escalating, the remaining harassed staff hadn't had time to work out any estimates. Costs were unknown, there were no facilities, no service department lay behind them and a parts cache hadn't even been thought of.

Much to the consternation of his staff who had been anticipating no more than five to ten cars in the first batch, O'Flaherty ordered 200 Beetles. When the Beetles arrived in consignments of 20, complete with £10 worth of spares and each allegedly finished in gleaming black, they were delivered to the newly appointed distributors as quickly as possible to avoid storage costs. Each one had to take a minimum of four cars plus, in true VW-style, £250-worth of spares and £100-worth of tools.

According to someone heavily involved at the time, the demands placed on the new dealers were kept as low as possible, so that they might not be 'scared off'. Nevertheless, whereas British manufactures were prepared to present anything between 17.5 and 20% discount to their dealers, Volkswagen offered and got away with, just a little over 16.5%.

By the end of 1953, J. J. Graydon (Dear's replacement) who had taken on responsibility for sales, had notched up a grand-total of 945 cars sold. Sadly, the company incurred a loss of £4,024, which under the circumstances was perhaps inevitable. The Beetle retailed at £649 19s 2d for the Standard or base model, £739 4s 2d for the Deluxe and £773 4s 2d for the Deluxe model with a sunroof. Each total included a hefty chunk of crippling Purchase Tax, with the basic price of the Deluxe for example amounting to a mere £521, but with £218 4s 2d extra added in tax.

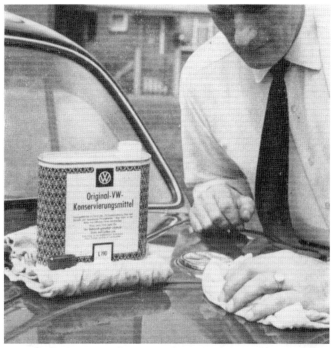

Left: *Accessory listings were just as popular in the 1960s as they are now. The photographs taken from an undated brochure, most likely produced around 1963-4, illustrate a few of the best sellers, some of which were produced exclusively for VW Motors Ltd, rather than being supplied courtesy of Wolfsburg. Curiously no price was given for the polish shown in the top picture, but one suitable for all chrome cost 4s 6d. The mud-flaps were available in two colour-ways! For the pair pictured (bottom) a customer would expect to pay £1 9s 6d, while for a white set with a black embossed VW symbol the price shot up to £2 0s 3d.*

In those early days, reports in British motoring press were full of praise for the Beetle, with attributes (that in later years would be the subject of criticism) receiving nothing but praise. In a report dated March 1954 *Light Car* wrote of "unobtrusive' engine noise, while 'full marks' could be 'awarded to the heater unit." The conclusion glowed with enthusiasm:- "In the Volkswagen we have an ingenious and practical approach to the economy car. It offers space, performance, excellent finish and, we should say, a long, trouble-free life." The writer of *The Motor's* 1954 road test was equally complimentary. "In all, this Volkswagen justifies its aim as a people's car and has very considerable appeal to the enthusiast as well … it is easy to understand its ever-growing popularity."

Happily, perhaps in part due to the press reports, 1954 saw an increase in sales of close on 350%, or 3,260 cars sold, while, for the next two years the figures hovered just above the 5,000 mark. In 1958 they saw a lift to 7436 sales and again in 1959, this time to 9,227. The picture in the 1960s was one of continued growth.

Inevitably, hostility to Volkswagen and its product gradually diminished. However, before the situation improved vandalism had became so bad at one stage that discussions with Nordhoff ensued and a three-month timescale for improvement was fixed before a decision would have been taken to abandon imports altogether. At the point when three out of every four cars delivered were being attacked the damage ranged from blows with hammers or spanners on door panels to much more malicious acts, such as placing batteries upside-down on floor pans to cause acid leakage and damage.

Another restricting factor in the early days was the system of import quotas operated by the Board of Trade. Briefly, an overall annual figure was arrived at, with each importer being allocated a proportionate amount. A problem arose when some failed to take up their options while others, Volkswagen included, were desperate for more. This situation was eventually resolved before the system was abolished in 1958, but other hindrances in the form of higher custom duties, surcharges and additional taxes were always waiting in the wings.

Even Wolfsburg's overwhelming success was a potential threat to the British concession as at one point VW informed Graydon and his colleagues that, owing to world demand, they were unable to supply any more cars for the time being.

travelled to VW's headquarters and met with Nordhoff, who in turn immediately instigated Saturday working in order to satisfy the requirements from the British market.

Although the concession was growing and the numbers of problems were diminishing, it was still apparent that if Volkswagen Motors Limited was to become a truly major player, in line with Volkswagen operations elsewhere, a great deal more capital was required.

In 1957, Volkswagen Motors Ltd. became a cog in the Thomas Tilling group of companies. Although Britain would eventually become Volkswagen's fourth largest market, after the USA, Germany of course and Brazil, the progression from poor to adequate and eventually excellent sales was relatively slow when compared to other 'conquered' countries.

As the 1960s dawned Volkswagen Motors could account for in excess of 36,000 VWs on British roads, which was hardly sensational but was certainly encouraging. However, by 1963 the company was able to celebrate its 100,000 sale, most of which had been derived from the Beetle. Such was their joy that Volkswagen Motors Ltd presented Lord Montagu with a 1953 Beetle, which he added to the National Motor Museum collection. Annual sales within a 10-year timescale had grown to the best part of 30,000 a year, while the company could boast of being the largest car importer to British shores.

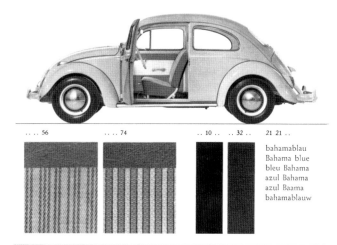

Top Right: *The paint shades available, together with upholstery options, led to a separate piece of print, although not necessarily specific to the British market. This 1964 colour publication shows the shades available as Ruby Red, Black, Pearl White, Sea Blue (almost a petrol blue), Panama Beige, Java Green (a green with a most definite hint of blue), Anthracite (a darkish grey) and Bahama Blue (a pale tone of blue with a hint of green).*

Middle Right: *The number of options for the British market tended to be less than for the home market, but as a result of a Europe-wide recession which hit hard in 1967, when Nordhoff introduced the 'Sparkafer', or 'budget Beetle' in Germany, he added a low specification 1200 Beetle to the models available in the UK. The car was basic certainly, but not primitive like the Standard models of old, which had finally disappeared from the listings as such in the mid-Sixties. Nordhoff's timely message to a 'strapped for cash' public was: 'VW 1200 – A car which is economical through and through'.*

Bottom Right: *Within a few short years, Volkswagen established itself in Britain as a 'company' offering quality, reliability and longevity to prospective and established customers. Ever helpful, VW issued a yearly contact list of all authorised distributors and dealers. This version, dating from 1962, still made use of the Reuters's artwork.*

IN CONCLUSION

The majority of the photographs featured in this book are the work of Ken Cservenka, an avid VW enthusiast for more years than he might care to remember. His collection of pictures amounts to in excess of 600-boxes of slides, some of which date back to the Seventies, when the cars described were either only a few years old, or certainly hadn't achieved cherished status.

Author, Richard Copping's interest in the marque started before he had even learned to drive when a Bentley owning schoolmaster turned up one day in a Beetle! Having passed his test in a VW, in 1978 he purchased one of the last Beetles to be produced for the British market, a car he still owns today.

Above: *This is one of Ken's favourite daily-driver Beetles, an Anthracite Deluxe dating from the early 1960s. Nowadays Ken is the owner of a VW Camper van, plus a Standard model Beetle dating from 1956, which is awaiting restoration. Everyday transport comes in the form of one of VWs more recent water-cooled offerings. Ken attends most of the classic VW shows held each summer, where he can invariably be seen adding to his photographic collection.*

Richard's 'historic' VW is pictured on page 45, although this car is only used in the summer months. In recent years, his daily transport might not have been an air-cooled car, but it still wears with pride the famous 'V' over 'W' badge on its bodywork.